Jordanian Cooking

Step by Step

Distributed by:
Radwan Book Shop
Aqaba - Jordan
Tel.: +962 3 2013704
Fax: +962 3 2015588
Email: redwanbook@hotmail.com

Supervision:
Lina Bassam Chebaro
Nada Mosbah Halawani

Editing:
Lina Bassam Chebaro
Ghada Yamout Ramadan
Jamila Dandan
Nicole Awad

Food Preparation & Garnishing
Goodies Cuisine

Photoghraphy
Photo Naji

Desktop Publishing:
Abjad Graphics

Printing:
Mediterranean Press

 الدار العربية للعلوم
Arab Scientific Publishers

Reem Bldg., Sakiat Al-Janzir, Ain Al-Tenah, P.O.Box: 13/5574 - Beirut-Lebanon
Tel/Fax: 811373 - 860138 - 786233 - 785107 - 786607

Jordanian Cooking

Step by Step

Contents

Jordanian Cooking

Step by Step

75
Vegetables

119
Fish

90
Poultry

126
Beverages

103
Meat

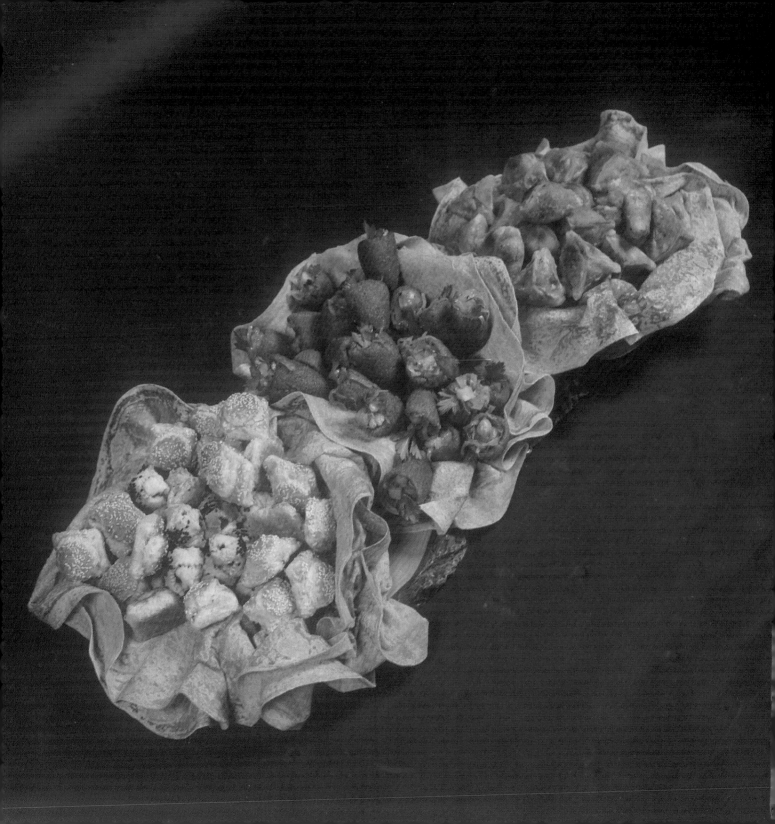

Introduction

For thousands of years, the Middle East has played a siginficant part in history as a trading link between East and West. Its dishes have developed through the wide variety of foods carried by the caravans and diversity of societies encountered through trade.

Using this book, you can become a Jordanian Chef, and taste the splendors and richness of the Jordanian cuisine! Also, discover over 100, step-by-step recipes each with a ready made photo. The recipes have been prepared in cooperation with the famous caterers "Goodies". This book includes 12 sections on salads, appetizers, pastries , soups, rice, grains, vegetables, chicken, meat, fish, pickles, and beverages; plus detailed basics, glossary and easy to use help. More than 300 photographs are included providing the reader with all the information he or she needs. Moreover, pictures describing the harder-to-prepare recipes, like pastries, kibbi balls, and stuffed vine leaves is included.

Lina Chebaro

Basic Dough

Al ajeena al assasiya

Serves: 8
Preparation time: 25 minutes

Ingredients:

1 kg (32 oz/5 cups) plain flour
1 ¼ cups tepid water
½ cup olive oil
½ cup vegetable oil
2 tablespoons salt
2 tablespoons sugar

Steps:

1) Sift the flour into a working surface.
2) Mix in salt and sugar. Make a well in the centre.
3) Pour olive oil and vegetable oil in the well.
4) Mix the dry ingredients into the liquid.
5) Add water gradually. Knead the dough into a ball (if the dough is too stiff add some water).
6) Knead the dough on a floured working surface until it is smooth and elastic this can be done in an electric mixer fitted with a dough hook, or in a food processor.
7) Form the dough into a ball and put into a lightly floured bowl, covered with a damp cloth. Leave in a warm place until the dough has doubled in size - about 6 hours.

Dairies

Makes: 8 cups of yoghurt or ½ kg (16 oz) strained yoghurt

Ingredients:

8 cups milk
½ cup yoghurt
1 teaspoon salt (as desired)

Yoghurt

Steps:

1) Bring milk to a boil. Place aside until tepid.
2) Stir in yoghurt. Cover pot with lid. Wrap pot with a wool cover. Place in a warm place for 6 hours.
3) Remove lid. Stir in salt. Cool in refrigerator for 3 hours.

Strained Yoghurt

Steps:

1) Pour the cold yoghurt into a cheese cloth bag.
2) Tie and let hang for 12 hours.

Note: You should double the time of straining the yoghurt when you double the quantity of yoghurt.

Cooked Yoghurt

Ingredients:

1 1/2 kg (48 oz) plain yoghurt
2 tablespoons cornstarch
1 teaspoon salt
1 cup water
1 beaten egg (or egg's white)

Steps:

1) Strain yoghurt using a smooth colander into a pot. Add egg or egg's white.
2) Dissolve cornstarch in 1 cup of water. Stir into cold yoghurt for 2 minutes.
3) Place on medium heat, stirring constantly until it boils.
4) Remove from heat and use as desired.

Preparing Nuts

Sesame:

Buy toasted or toast without butter or oil.

Pine Nuts:

Remove any impurities. Fry in some oil.

Almonds:

a) Soak almonds in boiling water for 20 minutes.
b) Remove, peel, and flake.
c) Wash then drain well. Fry in some oil.

Peanuts:

Toast in a pan without oil. Remove and place aside until cool. Peel and flake.

Pistachio Nuts:

Soak in boiling water for 20 minutes.

Remove, peel and flake. Wash, drain well, and then fry in some oil.

Walnuts:

Soak in cold water for about 1 hour or until lighter in color. Wash well, drain, and then fry in some oil.

Cashews:

Wash well. Drain then fry in some oil.

Hazelnuts:

Toast in an oven or in a pan without oil. Remove, place aside until cool, peel, and flake.

Parsley Salad
Tabbouleh

The most famous salad, made of: parsley, tomato, mint and burghul.

Serves: 5

Preparation time: 40 minutes

Ingredients:

¹/₄ cup burghul, fine cracked wheat
2 cups finely chopped parsley
¹/₂ kg (16 oz) firm red tomatoes, washed and
  finely chopped
¹/₂ cup finely chopped fresh mint leaves
¹/₄ cup finely chopped onion
¹/₂ cup lemon juice
1 teaspoon salt (as desired)
¹/₂ cup extra virgin olive oil
a dash of all spice (as desired)

Steps:

1. Wash chopped mint and parsley then drain well.
2. Wash the burghul several times and drain. Soak in chopped tomatoes for 20 minutes.
3. Rub chopped onion with salt. Mix all ingredients in a bowl. Add olive oil and lemon juice, toss the mixture well.
4. Serve Tabbouleh with crisp cos lettuce leaves, or fresh cabbage leaves.

Beetroot and Sesame Paste Salad

Salatet al shamandar bil-tahini

This salad is usually served with seafood.

Serves: 5

Preparation time: about 20 minutes

Cooking time: 1 hour

Ingredients:

1 kg (32 oz) beetroots, boiled till tender (about 1 hour)
¹/₂ cup sesame paste
¹/₂ cup lemon juice
1 tablespoon finely chopped fresh parsley
1 teaspoon salt (as desired)

Steps:

1. Peel beetroots and cut into cubes.
2. Blend well sesame paste, salt, lemon juice and parsley. Adjust taste by water or lemon juice.
3. Pour over beetroot cubes and mix to coat.
4. Serve it as a side dish with fish.

Note: You can add minced onion to this salad. You can also substitute beetroots with boiled and chopped swisschard's stems.

Thyme Salad

Salatet al zaatar alakhdar

A tasty appetizer.

Serves: 2
Preparation time: 15 minutes

Ingredients:

1 bunch thyme
¹/₄ cup lemon juice
¹/₄ teaspoon salt
2 tablespoons olive oil
1 small onion, finely chopped

Steps:

1. Pick thyme leaves, wash well, drain, squeeze with your hands.
2. Rub onion well with salt in a bowl. Mix with lemon juice and olive oil. Add to thyme and toss well.
3. Serve accompanied by different grills.

Note: Adding 1 tablespoon of pomegranate thickened juice to this salad would give a special taste.

Broad Beans and Artichoke Salad

Salatet al Foul wal Ardi Chawki

A delicious and easy to prepare salad.

Serves: 4
Preparation time: 10 minutes

Ingredients:

500 g (16 oz) artichoke (canned)
1 cup green broad beans, peeled
¹/₄ cup lemon juice
¹/₄ cup olive oil
2 cloves garlic, crushed with a dash of salt

Steps:

1. Wash aritchoke. Halve.
2. Place broad beans in centre of a serving bowl. Arrange the artichoke halves around it.
3. Mix well garlic, lemon juice, and olive oil. Sprinkle lemon juice mixture over the broad beans and artichoke.

Cucumber and Yoghurt Salad

Salatet al laban bil khyar

A tasty refreshing salad, best served with rice dishes.

Serves: 6

Preparation time: about 20 minutes

Ingredients:

500 (16 oz) cucumbers, diced
3 cups yoghurt
3 cloves garlic, crushed with a dash of salt
1 teaspoon salt (as desired)
1 teaspoon dried ground mint
1 cup water

Steps:

1. Blend well yoghurt and water till consistent.
2. Add cucumber, garlic, salt and mint. Blend well.
3. Serve cold.

Lima Beans Salad

Salatet al fasoulya al bayda

This appetizer is usually served with main dishes.

Serves: 5

Preparation time: about 1 hour

Cooking time: 45 minutes

Ingredients:

2 cups Lima beans (soaked for 1 night)
2 cloves garlic, crushed with a dash of salt
¹/₄ cup lemon juice
¹/₂ cup finely chopped fresh parsley
¹/₂ cup extra virgin olive oil
¹/₂ teaspoon salt

Steps:

1. Wash beans and drain. Add water to cover. Bring to a boil over medium heat. Reduce heat to low. Cover and simmer for 45 minutes or till tender.
2. Dressing: Mix well salt, garlic, lemon juice, oil and parsley.
3. Drain beans and pour dressing over.
4. Serve hot or cold.

Toasted Bread Salad

Al Fattoush

A delicious salad containing toasted bread, parsley, tomato and other vegetables.

Serves: 5
Preparation time: 30 minutes

Ingredients:

$^1/_2$ *Lebanese round bread (pitta), toasted*
3 medium firm tomatoes, washed and chopped
3 slender cucumbers (250g/19 oz), washed and chopped
3 medium radishes (250g/19 oz) (1 cup), washed and chopped
4 spring onions, washed and coarsely chopped
1 medium onion ($^1/_4$ cup), roughly chopped
$^1/_2$ *cup lemon juice*
2 cloves garlic, crushed with a pinch of salt
$^1/_2$ *teaspoon dried mint*
2 tablespoons vinegar
$^1/_2$ *cup olive oil*
1 cup coarsely chopped fresh mint leaves
1 cup coarsely chopped parsley
1 cup small purslane leaves
$^1/_2$ *teaspoon ground sumac*
$^1/_2$ *cup coarsely chopped sweet green pepper*
1 teaspoon salt
8 crisp cos (2 cups) lettuce leaves, torn into bite size pieces
$^1/_2$ *Lebanease round pitta bread, toasted (extra)*

Steps:

1. Break toasted bread into small pieces and keep aside.
2. Wash the chopped mint, parsley and purslane, then drain well.
3. Mix crushed garlic with salt, oil, vinegar, dried mint, lemon juice and ground sumac and keep aside.
4. Put all ingredients in a serving bowl. Add toasted bread pieces and dress with garlic mixture, mix well.
5. Serve fattoush if you wish garnished with additional toasted bread.

Mixed Green Salad

Salatet al khoudar al moonawa

A nutritious salad.

Serves: 4
Preparation time: 30 minutes

Ingredients:

¹/₂ kg (16 oz) red tomatoes, cubed
¹/₂ kg (16 oz) cucumbers, cut into rounds
¹/₂ medium Cos lettuce, broken into small pieces
1 green sweet pepper, coarsely chopped
1 medium sized onion, coarsely chopped
¹/₂ bunch purslane leaves, washed
¹/₂ cup fresh mint leaves, washed
3 cloves garlic crushed with a dash of salt
¹/₄ cup olive oil
¹/₄ cup lemon juice
1 tablespoon pomegranate thickened juice (optional)
1 teaspoon salt (as desired)

Steps:

1. Put all vegetables in a bowl. Mix garlic, olive oil, lemon juice, salt and pomegranate juice. Add to vegetables, toss well.
2. Serve immediately accompanied by different dishes.

Fried Omelet Balls

Akras al iggi al maklia

Delicious omelet balls of eggs and vegetables.

Serves: 4

Preparation time: 30 minutes

Frying time: 30 minutes

Ingredients:

¹/₂ cup fresh parsley, washed and finely chopped
6 eggs
¹/₂ cup finely chopped onion
¹/₄ cup plain flour
2 medium zucchini, finely chopped
1 sweet pepper, washed and grated
¹/₂ teaspoon salt (as desired)
¹/₄ teaspoon ground allspice (as desired)
¹/₄ teaspoon ground chili pepper
¹/₄ teaspoon baking powder
lemon zest
2 cups vegetable oil

Steps:

1. Wash chopped parsley and drain well. Mix chopped onions, salt, spices, parsley, chopped sweet pepper, and zucchini.
2. In another bowl, mix flour with baking powder then add to vegetable mixture. Blend eggs in a separate bowl, stir-in lemon zest. Add the mixture to vegetable mixture and stir.
3. Heat oil in a pan, pour in a spoonful of omelet.
4. Turn over each ball till it is golden-brown from both sides (repeat the process with the remaining mixture).
5. Serve balls warm with salad and fried potatoes.

Note: you can substitute whole zucchini with its cores.

Eggplant with Sesame Paste

Motabal al bathinjan

A sensational appetizer that is served with most meals.

Serves: 5

Preparation time: 30 minutes

Cooking time: 15 minutes

Ingredients:

2 large eggplants, about 1 kg (32 oz)
¼ cup lemon juice (as desired)
¼ cup sesame seed paste
3 cloves garlic crushed with ½ tablespoon salt (as desired)
1 teaspoon white vinegar
2 tablespoons parsley, finely chopped

Steps:

1. Grill eggplants on high heat for 15 minutes after piercing them by a fork on all sides. Turning frequently.
2. When tender, wash under running water then peel off skin while hot and remove stem. Pound to a purée (use a food processor, if available). Blend in gradually sesame paste, lemon juice, and vinegar. When mixture is consistent, add garlic and beat mixture well. If thick, adjust by lemon juice and water.
3. Serve it garnished with parsley, red pepper and olive oil.

Eggplant Casserole
Msakaet al bathinjan (al magmour)

An exotic appetizer. Try it.

Serves: 5
Preparation time: 30 minutes
Cooking time: 30 minutes

Ingredients:

1 kg (32 oz) eggplants, peeled and thickly cut,
* lengthwise*
1 kg (32 oz) tomatoes, peeled and sliced
1 cup of dried chickpeas, cooked (see p.9) or
* canned, washed and drained*
1 cup of quartered and sliced onion
2 tablespoons ground dried mint
10 cloves garlic, fried in oil
6 cloves garlic, crushed with a dash of salt
2 cups vegetable oil (or to cover eggplants)
1 teaspoon salt (as desired)
a dash of sugar
1 fresh red or green chili

Steps:

1. Sprinkle salt over eggplant slices. Fry eggplants till golden brown and drain on paper towels.
2. Fry onion rings until soft. Stir in garlic until golden.
3. Add tomatoes, chickpeas, chili, salt and sugar. Bring to a boil for 5 minutes.
4. Add fried eggplants. Cover pot, cook on moderate heat for 10 minutes.
5. Mix dry mint with crushed garlic. Add mint mixture to pot. Cook for 2 minutes.
6. Remove chili and serve cold with main dishes.

Chickpeas Purée

Hummus bil tahini

It is the number one appetizer in the Middle East.

Serves: 4

Preparation time: 30 minutes

Ingredients:

1 cup cooked chickpeas (see p. 9) or canned
1/2 teaspoon salt
2 cloves garlic, crushed with a pinch of salt
1/4 cup lemon juice
2 tablespoons sesame paste
2 tablespoons parsley, finely chopped
1/2 teaspoon ground cumin

Steps:

1. Drain warm chickpeas and reserve 1 tablespoon. Beat chickpeas in a food processor.
2. Blend chickpeas with the sesame paste, lemon juice, crushed garlic, and salt into a purée. Adjust flavor and consistency with lemon juice and salt if necessary (Hummus should be thick and smooth).
3. Serve in Hummus bowls. Pour olive oil in center and garnish with the reserved chickpeas, chopped parsley and cumin.

Potato with Coriander
Batata harra

A delicious appetizer of fried potatoes with fresh coriander.

Serves: 4

Preparation time: 15 minutes

Cooking time: 30 minutes

Ingredients:

1 kg (32 oz) potatoes
2 cups vegetable oil (for frying)
4 cloves garlic, crushed with a pinch of salt
1 teaspoon salt (as desired)
¹/₂ teaspoon ground red pepper (as desired)
2 tablespoons finely chopped fresh coriander
a dash of dried coriander

Steps:

1. Wash the fresh coriander, drain and put on a clean piece of cloth to dry (5 minutes). Peel the potatoes, wash and cut into small cubes, rewash and drain.
2. Fry the potatoes in hot oil until golden-brown, put on absorbent paper.
3. Mix the garlic with salt and fry in hot oil for 5 minutes till fragrant. Add to it the potatoes, a dash of dry coriander, and the red pepper.
4. Stir well for 2 minutes. Stir in fresh coriander then remove from heat.
5. Serve hot.

Grilled Kafta

Arayes

You can serve it as an appetizer or as a light meal. Delicious and easy to prepare.

Serves: 3
Preparation time: 25 minutes
Cooking time: 5 minutes

Ingredients:

$^1/_2$ **kg (16 oz) kafta (see p.176, step 1)**
1 $^1/_2$ pitta bread, cut into 12 pieces
2 tablespoons butter

Steps:

1. Spread some butter on the inner part of bread pieces.
2. Divide kafta into 12 portions. Spread over buttered bread.
3. Put the pieces in a grill or an oven at 200°C/400°F for 5 minutes or till kafta is cooked.
4. Serve hot with yoghurt.

Grilled Eggplants with Bell Pepper

Al rahib (baba ganooj)

A delicious appetizer for all times.

Serves: 5
Preparation time: 30 minutes

Ingredients:

1 kg (32 oz) grilled eggplants, washed then peeled
1 green bell pepper, finely chopped
1 medium onion, finely chopped
3 cloves of garlic, crushed with a dash of salt
¹/₂ kg (16 oz) tomatoes, peeled and finely chopped
¹/₂ cup lemon juice
1 teaspoon salt
a dash of olive oil

Steps:

1. Process eggplants until smooth
2. Stir in all the above ingredients.
3. Serve in a platter garnished with olive oil and green bell pepper slices.

Dandelion Leaves in Oil

Hindbeh bi-zayt

Perfect for hot summer lunches.

Serves: 5
Preparation time: 30 minutes
Cooking time: 30 minutes

Ingredients:

1 kg (32 oz) dandelion
$1/2$ cup olive oil
1 cup finely chopped parsley
5 onions ($1/2$ kg/16 oz) sliced into thin rings
3 garlic cloves crushed with a sprinkle of salt
$1/2$ tablespoon salt (as desired)
a dash of bicarbonate of soda

Steps:

1. Remove yellow leaves from dandelion. Wash well. Finely chop.
2. Bring water to a boil then add bicarbonate of soda and dandelion and cook over medium heat for 5 minutes.
3. Drain and rinse in cold water, then squeeze until dry.
4. Fry onion until golden. Remove $1/2$ quantity of onions from oil, reserve aside. Fry chopped leaves in the same oil with onions for 15 minutes. Add garlic, coriander and salt and fry for 5 minutes.
5. Place in a serving plate and garnish with the reserved onions. Serve cold with some lemon juice.

Chickpeas in Oil

Humus bil zayt (hummus balila)

Usually this dish is prepared for breakfast when all the family members are around.

Serves: 3
Preparation time: 20 minutes
Soaking time: 12 hours

Ingredients:

1 cup cooked chickpeas or canned chickpeas
2 tablespoons lemon juice
¼ cup olive oil
4 tablespoons butter
1 teaspoon ground cumin (as desired)
1 teaspoon ground cinnamon (as desired)
½ cup pine nuts, fried
2 cloves garlic, crushed with a dash of salt

Steps:

1. Drain warm chickpeas. Put in a bowl. Mix with garlic, lemon juice, ½ teaspoon of cumin, cinnamon and melted butter.
2. Garnish with pine nuts and ½ teaspoon of cumin and olive oil.
3. Serve with tomatoes and green onions.

Chick Peas in Yoghurt

Fattet al hummus

It is a very tasty and popular dish. You can serve it as an appetizer or as a breakfast.

Serves: 5
Preparation time: 30 minutes

Ingredients:

$^1/_2$ kg (16 oz) (2 cups) canned chickpeas
5 cups yoghurt
5 cloves garlic, crushed with a dash of salt
2 tablespoons sesame paste
1 teaspoon salt (as desired)
1 toasted pita bread (30 cm in diameter)
3 tablespoons fried pine nuts
$^1/_2$ teaspoon ground cumin
$^1/_2$ teaspoon ground red pepper (as desired)
$^1/_4$ cup melted butter for garnishing
1 teaspoon vinegar
$^1/_2$ medium size pomegranate
8 cups water
$^1/_2$ teaspoon bicarbonate of soda

Steps:

1. Blend well yoghurt, garlic, salt, vinegar and sesame paste.
2. Cut pita bread into small pieces. Place in a deep dish.
3. Put hot chickpeas with its liquid (about 2 cups) over the bread. Add yoghurt mixture.
4. Garnish with pine nuts, butter, pomegranate, pepper, and cumin. Serve hot.

Stuffed Eggplant with Yoghurt

Fattet al bathinjan

A famous Syrian dish. It consists of stuffed eggplants with yoghurt.

Serves: 5
Preparation time: 40 minutes
Cooking time: 50 minutes

Ingredients:

1 kg (32 oz) small eggplants
400 g (14 oz) minced meat
$^1/_2$ cup fried pine nuts
1 cup tomato juice or paste
2 tablespoons pomegranate thickened juice
1 cup water
1 teaspoon salt (as desired)
a dash of ground black pepper
a dash of ground cinnamon
4 cups yoghurt
6 cloves garlic crushed with a dash of salt
2 toasted pitta bread
2 cups vegetable oil (for frying the eggplants)
2 tablespoons butter (for frying minced meat)
2 tablespoons melted butter for garnishing

Steps:

1. Fry minced meat in butter then add peppers and salt. Mix well on low heat for 10 minutes. Put aside.
2. Roll eggplant on a surface, so that hollowing would be easier.
3. Wash eggplants well. Remove stem ends.
4. Hollow out with an apple corer. Wash well again. Drain.
5. Mix fried meat and half the quantity of pine nuts. Fill the eggplants with meat mixture. Fry the stuffed eggplants in oil then put aside.
6. Put tomato juice in a pan then add water, pomegranate and salt. Stir to mix.
7. Add the stuffed eggplants to the tomato mixture. Bring to a boil. Lower heat and leave for 40 minutes or until tender and $^1/_2$ cup of the liquid is left.
8. Cut toasted pita bread into small pieces. Put in a heavy based plate. Add eggplants and liquid. Mix yoghurt with garlic then add them to the plate.
9. Sprinkle the fried pine nuts and butter over the yoghurt. Serve hot.

Note: You can garnish this dish also with minced meat.

Broad Bean Patties
Falafel

The Egyptian and Lebanese kitchens are known for the delicious FALAFEL made mainly from beans.

Serves: 6
Preparation time: 1 hour 30 minutes
Cooking time: 30 minutes

Ingredients:

1 kg (32 oz) peeled green fava beans (dried)
1 cup roughly chopped fresh parsley
1 cup roughly chopped fresh coriander
3 heads garlic, peeled and crushed
3 large onions, chopped
1/2 teaspoon ground cinnamon
1/2 teaspoon ground cumin
2 teaspoons salt
1 teaspoon ground paprika
1 teaspoon ground chili
1/2 teaspoon ground black pepper
2 tablespoons plain flour
1 teaspoon ground dried coriander
1/2 teaspoon bicarbonate of soda
3 teaspoons baking powder
5 cups vegetable oil (for deep frying)

Steps:

1. Soak the beans in water for 24 hours, then drain well.
2. Mix all ingredients except (salt, cumin, cinnamon, paprika, black pepper, chili, bicarbonate, and baking powder).
3. Grind in a food processor.
4. Add to the mixture salt, peppers, bicarbonate, baking powder and process another time.
5. Leave mixture aside for 30 minutes then knead.
6. Divide mixture into balls using a special tool for Falafel balls, if this tool is not available take a spoonful of mixture and make flat balls. Heat oil in deep pan over high heat, then fry till browned.
7. Serve Falafel hot with parsley, tomatoes, fresh mint, spring onions, pickles and sesame paste.

Dried Fava Beans in Oil

Fool medammes

The most popular Arabian breakfast, almost every region has more than a restaurant specialized in serving this dish.

Serves: 3
Preparation time: 30 minutes
Soaking time: 24 hours

Ingredients:

1 cup cooked fava beans or canned fava beans
$^1/_2$ cup lemon juice
3 cloves garlic crushed with 1 teaspoon salt (as desired)
2 tablespoons finely chopped fresh parsley
$^1/_2$ cup olive oil

Steps:

1. Drain the warm fava beans. Put in a bowl. Mix garlic, lemon juice and $^1/_2$ quantity of oil. Add to beans and mix well.
2. Garnish with parsley and olive oil.
3. Serve with spring onions and tomatoes.

Stuffed Eggplants in Oil

Bathinjan bi-zayt

The best of stuffed vegetables.

Serves: 5
Preparation time: 1 hour
Cooking time: 1 hour

Ingredients:

1 kg (32 oz) small and long eggplants
¹/₄ cup finely chopped fresh mint leaves
¹/₂ cup finely chopped onion
1 kg (32 oz) finely chopped tomatoes
2 cups finely chopped parsley
1 cup olive oil and vegetable oil mixture
¹/₂ cup short grain rice
1 teaspoon salt (as desired)
¹/₂ cup lemon juice
a dash of ground white pepper
2 medium potatoes cut into slices
1 teaspoon pomegranate thickened juice (optional)
1 ¹/₂ cups water or to cover 3 cm above the stuffed eggplants
a dash of ground allspice
a dash of ground cinnamon

Steps:

1. Prepare filling as the Warak Enab Bi-Zayt.
2. Roll each eggplant between your hands to make hollowing out the eggplants easier.
3. Cut off eggplants stem ends, using a sharp knife.
4. Hollow using an apple corer or a special zucchini corer, removing the pulp and leaving a ³/₄ cm thick wall (be careful not to pierce walls).
5. Fill the eggplants with filling. Don't over stuff. Reserve filling's stock. Pour ¹/₂ cup of oil and arrange potato slices at the bottom of a pot. Lay side by side stuffed eggplants over the potato slices. Invert a plate on top of the eggplants.
6. Add lemon juice, filling's stock, pomegranate juice, water, and oil. Bring to a boil on high heat. Cover, reduce heat and simmer for one hour or until tender.
7. Serve cold garnished with potato slices.

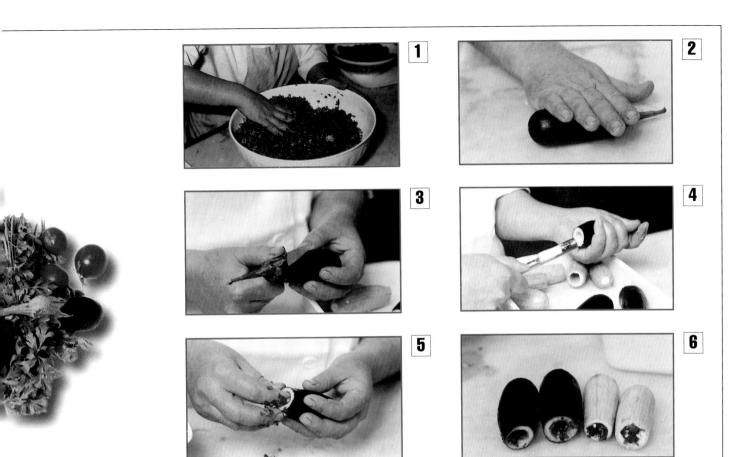

Stuffed Zucchini in Oil

Kousa Mahshou bi-zayt

Follow stuffed eggplant in oil recipe (see p. 32).

Raw Kibbi

Kibbi nayye

Kibbi is the main dish in the Levant. Whatever meat you use, trim of all fat and gristle before preparation.

Serves: 6
Preparation time: 30 minutes

Ingredients:

500 g (16 oz) ground lean beef or lamb
1 cup fine burghul
1 small onion, peeled
$1/2$ teaspoon ground allspice
$1/2$ teaspoon ground cinnamon
1 teaspoon salt (as desired)
1 tablespoon pine nuts and few fresh mint leaves
  for garnish
8 fresh basil leaves
8 fresh marjoram leaves
$1/4$ cup cleaned walnuts
Virgin olive oil

Steps:

1. Rinse burghul, drain in a sieve and press with back of spoon to remove as much moisture as possible. Strain again with your hands to make sure it is dry.
2. Process with onion, marjoram and basil.
3. Mix meat with burghul, salt, allspice and cinnamon. Dip your hands in cold water and knead the mixture. Keep your hands wet. Knead till mixture is firm and smooth.
4. Place on platter and shape into a flat round. Dip hands into cold water and smooth all over.
5. Serve garnished with pine nuts, walnuts, mint leaves and some virgin olive oil.

Note: If you desire piquant raw kibbi, add red dried hot chilies to burghul when processing it with onion, majoram, and basil.

Okra in Oil
Bamyi bi-zayt

A delicious appetizer.

Serves: 5
Preparation time: 15 minutes
Cooking time: 30 minutes

Ingredients:

700 g (1 ¹/₂ lb) fresh okra / frozen or canned, trim stem end and wash
1 kg (32 oz) tomatoes, washed and sliced
1 cup finely chopped onion
2 heads garlic, peeled
1 teaspoon salt (as desired)
¹/₂ cup vegetable oil or olive oil
1 cup finely chopped fresh coriander, washed
1 tablespoon ground dried coriander
4 cloves garlic, crushed
1 fresh red or green chili
1 cup water
a dash of ground allspice
a dash of sugar

Steps:

1. Fry okra in oil. Remove and put on paper towels.
2. Fry onions in oil till transparent. Add dried coriander and garlic. Stir for 2 minutes till fragrant.
3. Add tomatoes. Cook over medium heat for another 2 minutes.
4. Add okra, salt, sugar, allspice, chili, and water. Bring to a boil over medium heat and cook for 25 minutes or till okra is tender. Add fresh coriander and boil for 2 minutes.

Seasoned Brains
Nikhaat bil hamod wal-zayt

A very nutritious appetizer.

Serves: 3
Preparation time: 15 minutes
Cooking time: 20 minutes

Ingredients:

3 sheep's brain
1 large onion, peeled and halved
1 lemon wedge
1 cinnamon stick
a dash of salt
3 cloves garlic, crushed with a dash of salt
$^1/_2$ cup lemon juice
olive oil
3 bay leaves

Steps:

1. Remove the thin membrane of the brain under running water. Place in a pot. Cover with water. Add a dash of salt, cinnamon sticks, onion, and lemon wedge.
2. Bring to a boil over moderate heat. Skim off scum and remove lemon wedge. Leave on heat for 10 minutes.
3. Drain the brains. Wash under running cold water. Drain well and place in plate.
4. Add salt, garlic, lemon juice, and a dash of olive oil.
5. Serve garnished with radishes.

Fried Liver

Kibed makli

*A **nutritious** appetizer served before a main meal or as a brunch.*

Serves: 5
Preparation time: 15 minutes
Cooking time: 20 minutes

Ingredients:

¹/₂ kg (16 oz) chicken liver, small cubes (remove thin transparent layer)
3 large onions, sliced
¹/₂ teaspoon salt (as desired)
¹/₂ teaspoon ground hot black pepper (as desired)
¹/₂ teaspoon ground allspice
¹/₂ cup lemon juice or 2 tablespoons pomegranate juice or 1 tablespoon balsamic vinegar
2 tablespoons butter

Steps:

1. Fry onion with butter on medium heat until golden.
2. Add liver cubes, salt and spices. Stir occasionally, for 10 minutes or until tender.
3. Pour lemon juice or pomegranate, mix gently and cook for 2 minutes.
4. Serve hot with lemon wedges.

Stuffed Grape Vine Leaves in Oil

Warak Enab Bi-Zayt

It is considered the best appetizer by everybody.

Serves: 5
Preparation time: 1 hour
Cooking time: 1 hour

Ingredients:

500 g (16 oz) grape vine leaves
4 cups (4 bunches) finely chopped fresh parsley
$1/4$ cup finely chopped fresh mint
$1/2$ cup short grain rice
1 kg (32 oz) finely chopped tomatoes
1 teaspoon salt
  a dash of allspice
1 cup olive oil and vegetable oil mixture
2 medium onions, finely chopped
3 cups water
2 medium potatoes, peeled and sliced into rounds
$3/4$ cup lemon juice
1 teaspoon pomegranate thickened juice (optional)
a dash of ground cinnamon
a dash of ground white pepper

Steps:

1. Filling: Rub onions with salt. Mix rice with onion, mint, tomato and parsley. Stir in $1/2$ quantity of lemon juice, $1/2$ quantity of olive oil, salt, and spices.
2. Snip off vine leaves stems if necessary. Rinse in cold water and blanch in boiling water for 2 minutes in 3 or 4 lots. Remove with slotted spoon and place in cold water.
3. Place a vine leaf shiny side down on work surface.
4. Place about a tablespoon of stuffing near stem end.
5. Fold end and sides over stuffing and roll up firmly. Repeat the same process with the remaining leaves.
6. Place $1/2$ cup oil in a heavy pan line base of the heavy pan with potato rounds and pack vine leaves rolls close together in layers.
7. Invert a heavy plate on top to keep rolls in shape during cooking.
8. Add $1/2$ cup lemon juice , pomegranate juice, filling's stock and 3 cups water. Cover, bring to a boil over moderate heat. Reduce the heat and let simmer for one hour or until tender.
9. Serve cold, garnished with potato slices.

Green Pea Pastries

Oozi

One of the most popular and tasty pastries in Syria. It consists of rice, meat, and green peas.

Serves: 7
Preparation time: 30 minutes
cooking time: 1 hour

Ingredients:

2 cups rice
1 cup green peas
$\frac{1}{2}$ kg (16 oz) minced meat
2 tablespoons fried pine nuts
2 tablespoons blanched, fried almonds
500 g (16 oz) puff pastry
4 tablespoons shortening or butter
a dash of salt and pepper (as desired)
4 $\frac{1}{2}$ cups water
$\frac{1}{4}$ cup shortening or butter
1 egg, beaten with a dash of white pepper

Steps:

1. Fry minced meat in shortening with a dash of salt and pepper. Cook until tender. Drain and put aside.
2. Wash rice and soak for $\frac{1}{4}$ hour in lukewarm water. Fry peas for 5 minutes in the same shortening. Add 4$\frac{1}{2}$ cups of water, bring to a boil for 15 minutes. Add rice, salt, and pepper. Cover and cook for 25 minutes on low heat. Stir into cooked rice and peas: minced meat, almonds, and pine nuts.
3. Roll out puff pastry using a rolling pin.
4. Divide into equal squares.
5. Roll out each square so that it would fit in a small bowl.
6. Put 2 tablespoonfuls of rice mixture in the center of each square in the small bowl.
7. Brush sides of pastry with beaten egg.
8. Fold the sides over the rice mixture.
9. Press well in order to have a little bundle shape.
10. Arrange pastries in a greased oven tray. Brush pastries with beaten egg. Garnish with some pine nuts. Place tray in hot oven (200°C/400°F) till golden and cooked.

 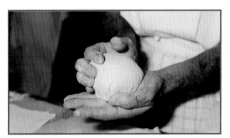

Vegetable Rolls
Rakaek bil khoudar

You can freeze these rolls, defrost and fry before serving.

Serves: 4
Preparation time: about 45 minutes
Cooking time: about 15 minutes

Ingredients:

8 filo pastries
1 cup grated carrots
³/₄ cup grated onions
1 cup thin cabbage strips
1 ¹/₄ cups vegetable oil
¹/₄ teaspoon salt

Steps:

1. Spread filo pastries, cut each in half in order to get 16 peices.
2. Fry all ingredients in ¹/₄ cup of oil for 5 minutes over low heat. Stir. Remove and put aside.
3. Put some vegetable mixture on the smooth side of each filo. Fold sides and roll neatly. Fry in hot oil over medium heat till golden-brown.
4. Serve hot.

Cheese Cigars

Rakaek bil jiben

Loved by children and adults at all times.

Serves: 4
Preparation time: 35 minutes
Cooking time: about 15 minutes

Ingredients:

8 sheets filo pastry
350 g (12 oz) white cheese, (al- ikawi al tishiki)
  grated
1/2 cup finely chopped fresh parsley
1/4 cup Mozzarella cheese, grated
1 egg beaten with a dash of white pepper
1 cup vegetable oil (for frying)

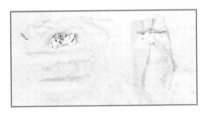

Steps:

1. Soak white cheese in water for 1 night. Change water occasionally. Drain.
2. Spread filo pastries. Cut in half. Place semi-circles over each other. Cut in half in order to get triangles.
3. Filling: Mix all ingredients except the vegetable oil.
4. Put some of the filling in the center of the smooth side of the filo pastries. Fold sides and roll neatly. Brush side with some flour dissolved in 1/4 cup of water to seal.
5. Fry in hot oil until golden. Serve hot with main dishes.

Meat-Cheese-Leek Pastries

Sambusik bilkarrath-jiben-lahem

Sambusik is usually served as an appetizer. It is an important part of meals in the Gulf.

Serves: 4

Preparation time: about 1 hour

Cooking time: about 35 minutes

Ingredients:

5 cups all purpose plain flour
1 1/2 cups lukewarm water
2 tablespoons salt
2 tablespoons sugar
vegetable oil for deep frying
1 cup oil

Cheese filling:
2 cups (425 g/14 oz) white cheese (Ikawi Altishiki), grated and salted (p 61)
1/4 cup finely chopped fresh parsley
1/4 teaspoon ground cayenne pepper

Meat filling:
300 g (10 oz) ground meat
1 tablespoon shortening or butter
1/4 cup fried pine nuts
a dash of ground allspice
1/4 teaspoon salt

Leek filling:
1/2 cup finely chopped onion
1 tablespoon shortening or butter
1 cup finely chopped leek
1/4 teaspoon salt
a dash of pepper

Steps:

1. Prepare dough: see p 8. Cover and leave aside for 1 hour.
2. Cheese filling: Mix ingredients and put aside.
   Meat filling: Fry meat in shortening, add salt, spices and pine nuts. Stir over medium heat for 1 minute. Put aside.
   Leek filling: Fry onion and leek in shortening. Add salt and pepper. Stir for 1 minute. Put aside.
3. Divide dough into walnut-size balls. Roll out to form circles (8 cm diameter).
4. Fill 1/3 the circles with cheese, another 1/3 with meat and the last 1/3 with leek following this way:

Put filling on one side of circle.
5. Fold over one end to make semi-circles.
6. Press edges with fingers.
7. Fry in 1 cup of vegetable oil over medium heat. Brown both sides.
8. Serve hot.

Note: 1) You can add ¹/₄ cup of chopped onion to meat filling.
2) You will get 25 pieces of every kind.

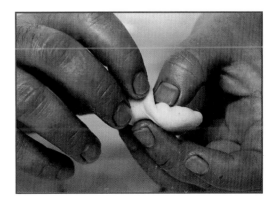

Meat Pastries in Yoghurt

Shishbarak

A main meal, delicious and nutritious.

Serves: 5
Preparation time (without dough): 1 hour 10 minutes
Cooking time: 20 minutes

Ingredients:

2 kg (64 oz) cooked yoghurt (see p 9)
½ quantity of basic dough recipe (see p 8)
3 cloves garlic, crushed with a dash of salt
1 cup finely chopped fresh coriander

Filling:
½ kg (16 oz) ground meat
3 medium sized onions, finely chopped
¼ cup fried pine nuts
1 teaspoon salt
¼ teaspoon ground allspice
¼ teaspoon ground cinnamon

Steps:

1. Roll out dough with a rolling pin to about 1 cm thickness.
2. Turn a coffee cup over, press over dough to get equal rounds.
3. Fry onion in shortening till color changes a little. Add meat, salt, allspice and cinnamon. Stir occasionally and fry for 10 minutes. Add pine nuts. Mix. Drain the mixture, butter would affect closing pastries.
4. Spread the round a little with your fingers.

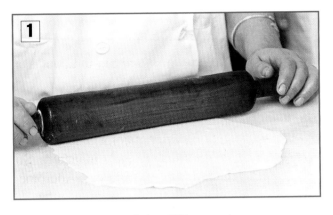

Place 1 teaspoon of the filling on it.

5. Fold over one end to make a semi-circle. Press edges down to seal.

6. Take the two ends from the straight side, bring them together to make a small ring. Press well. Repeat till rounds are done.

7. Place in a tray in a hot oven (200- 250°C/400- 525°F) for 10 minutes or until golden.

8. Add to boiling cooked yoghurt (see p.9) one by one. Let it boil over low heat for 10 minutes or till pastries are cooked.

9. Fry with shortening coriander and garlic. Add to cooked yoghurt mixture. Cook another 2 minutes.

10. Serve hot or cold with cooked rice.

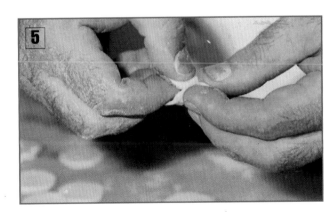

Spinach Pies

Fatayer bi sbanigh

An energetic appetizer.

Makes about: 40
Preparation time: about 45 minutes
Cooking time: 30 minutes

Dough Ingredients:

5 cups all purpose (plain) flour
1 tablespoon sugar
1 tablespoon salt
1 1/2 cups of water
1/4 cup vegetable oil

Filling:

1 1/2 kg (48 oz) fresh spinach
1/2 cup lemon juice
3 large onions, finely chopped
1 teaspoon salt
1 pinch of ground black pepper
2 tablespoons ground sumac (as desired)
1/4 cup vegetable oil
1 tablespoon pomegranate thickened juice (as desired)

Steps:

1. To prepare dough: (see p. 8) leave aside and cover for an hour to rise. Make sure dough doubles in volume.
2. Filling: Remove roots and yellow leaves from spinach. Chop finely then wash well and drain, rub with 1/2 teaspoon salt. Drain the spinach again with your hands to dry. Mash the onions with remaining salt. Add pepper and sumac. Add spinach to onion, then mix in oil and pomegranate. Put aside.
3. Roll out dough using a rolling pin till dough is as thin as possible (5 mm). Invert a tea cup on dough and press to have equal circles.
4. Place a tablespoon of spinach filling on each piece.
5. Bring up sides at 3 points to form a triangular shape.
6. Press edges firmly with fingertips to seal completely (put flour on finger tips to help seal).
7. Place pies on oiled baking sheets. Bake in a moderately hot oven (200°C/400°F) for 30 minutes.

Note: You can substitute spinach with unchopped purslane leaves.

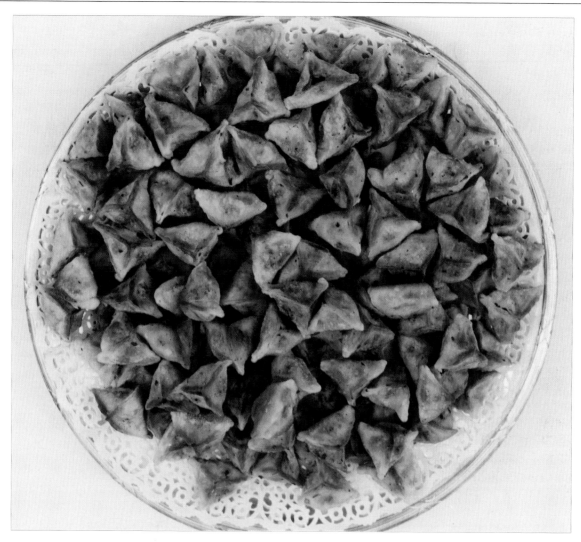

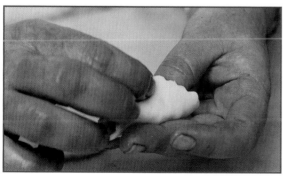

Meat Pastry Rolls

Lahem bi ajeen

Delicious meat pastries.

Makes: about 18
Preparation time: 1 hour
Cooking time: 30 minutes

Ingredients:

3 cups all purpose (plain) flour
1 egg
1 teaspoon salt
³/₄ cup water
4 cups vegetable oil

Filling:

400 g (14 oz) finely minced meat
3 onions, finely chopped
1 teaspoon salt
a dash of Lebanese ground 7 spices
2 tablespoons shortening or butter
2 tablespoons fried pine nuts
1 tablespoon ground sumac
1 tablespoon pomegranate thickened juice (if available)

Steps:

1. Mix flour, egg, salt, and water. Knead well, until dough is firm.
2. Put vegetable oil in a deep tray. Divide dough into small balls (walnut size). Put them in the tray and make sure they are covered with oil. Cover with a piece of texture and leave aside for 4 hours.
3. Fry onion in shortening until golden. Add minced meat, allspice and salt and fry over medium heat for 15 minutes. Stir, fried pine nuts, sumac, and pomegranate juice into meat. Preheat oven (200°C/400°F) for half an hour before you put the pastries.
4. Put one dough ball on an oiled board and spread it using your finger-tips to form a very thin rectangle.
5. Fold to form half a rectangle, then fold from right to left.
6. Place 1 tablespoon of filling across one side of the squares.
7. Fold the other side to cover filling, and press to close.
8. Arrange in an oven tray. Bake at (200°C/400°F) for 30 minutes.
9. Serve hot or cold with yoghurt or salads.

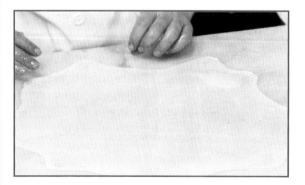
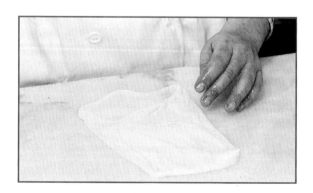

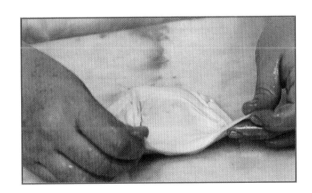

Meat Pastries

Baalbeck sfiha

One of the most famous Lebanese savoury pastries.

Serves: 5
Preparation time: 60 minutes
Cooking time: 30 minutes

Ingredients:

Dough, same recipe (see p. 8 exclude oil and add
1 teaspoon yeast dissolved in ¹/₄ cup water)
¹/₂ kg (16 oz) ground lamb meat
1 kg (32 oz) firm tomatoes, finely chopped
5 medium onions, finely chopped
1 teaspoon salt
a dash of: ground cayenne red pepper, ground
cinnamon, and ground allspice
2 tablespoons butter, diced
2 tablespoons yoghurt
1 tablespoon sesame paste (Tahinah)
1 tablespoon pomegranate thickened juice (if
available)
4 tablespoons fried pine nuts

Steps:

1. Mix well meat, tomatoes, onion and spices. Add yoghurt, sesame paste and pomegranate. Mix all with fried pine nuts. Add butter.
2. Divide dough into walnut size balls. Roll between hand palms to smooth.
3. Roll out balls with a rolling pin to form 8 cm diameter circles. Put one tablespoon of meat mixture on dough circle seeing that a cube is in each spoon.
4. Bring the edges up and press to make a square.
5. Arrange meat pastries in a tray brushed with butter. Bake in a moderate heat oven (180°C/350°F) for 30 minutes or till dough is golden and meat is cooked.
6. Serve hot with yoghurt.

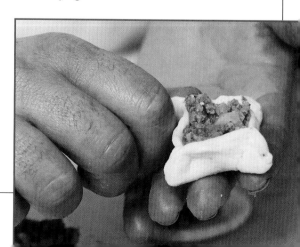

Thyme Pastries

Manakeesh bi zahtar

One of the most famous Lebanese pastries.

Serves: 4-6
Preparation time: 60 minutes
Cooking time: 15 minutes

Ingredients:

$^1/_2$ quantity basic dough recipe (exclude oil and add 1 teaspoon yeast dissolved in $^1/_4$ cup of water)
6 tablespoons thyme (zahtar)
$^1/_2$ cup olive oil

Steps:

1. Set oven at (250°C/525°F).
2. Divide dough into rounds. Cover with cloth for 15 minutes. Roll out each round to medium thickness (8 cm diameter) on floured board.
3. Place rounds on greased baking sheet. Mix zahtar and oil together. Spread mixture evenly over the rounds. Bake for 15 minutes in a moderately hot oven (180°C/350°F).
4. Serve for breakfast or for a snack.

Vegetable Soup

Hisaa al-khoudar

This soup has a variety of vegetables, added to either meat or chicken. It can be served as an appetizer or a light meal.

Serves: 5
Preparation time: about 40 minutes
Cooking time: 2 hours 30 minutes

Ingredients:

¹/₂ kg (16 oz) chicken or cubed stew lamb meat
1 kg (32 oz) red ripe tomatoes, peeled and finely chopped
1 cup frozen green peas
1 cup cubed carrots
1 cup cubed potatoes
1 cup cubed zucchini
¹/₂ cup finely chopped fresh parsley
1 medium sized onion, peeled
¹/₂ cup roughly chopped string beans
¹/₂ tablespoon salt (as desired)
¹/₄ teaspoon ground black pepper
2 tablespoons butter
¹/₄ cup rice
2 ¹/₂ litres water

Steps:

1. Fry meat in butter until brown.
2. Add meat with onion, spices and salt to a pot filled with water. Cover and simmer for 2 hours or till tender.
3. Add vegetables and rice to meat. Cover and cook on medium heat for 30 minutes.
4. Add parsley. Remove from heat. Serve with main dishes with toasted bread.

Note: If you choose chicken, cook it for 40 minutes then remove bones.

Chicken Soup

Hisaa al dajaj

It is one of the hearty world known soups. All soups keep well, under refrigeration. They retain their full flavor when reheated.

Serves: 6

Preparation time: 20 minutes

Cooking time: 1 hour

Ingredients:

1 kg (32 oz) chicken, cut into 4 pieces
½ cup broken vermicelli
1 medium sized onion, peeled
2 tablespoons chopped celery or chopped fresh parsley
2 tablespoons shortening or butter
½ tablespoon salt (as desired)
2 ½ litres (10 cups) water
2 cinnamon sticks
1 cardamom pod -1 clove -1 nutmeg

Steps:

1. Fry the chicken in shortening for 7 minutes. Add 2 ½ liters of water, onion and solid spices and cook over medium heat for 40 minutes, or till tender.
2. Remove skin and bones from chicken pieces and cut meat into small cubes. Strain stock. Return cubes to stock.
3. Add celery, vermicelli and salt to stock and bring to a boil.
4. Simmer over low heat for 20 minutes. Serve hot.

Spinach with Fried Kibbi Balls Soup

Hisaa al sbanekh ma akras al-kibbi al moshamaa

*A **nutritious** soup rich with minerals.*

Serves: 4
Preparation time: 30 minutes
Cooking time: 30 minutes

Ingredients:

*250 g (8 oz) finely chopped trimmed spinach,
  washed and drained*
6 cups water
*10 kibbi balls baked for 10 minutes in a moderate
  heat oven*
2 tablespoons finely chopped fresh coriander
1 teaspoon salt
a dash of ground allspice
2 tablespoons shortening or butter
1 medium onion, finely chopped
3 cloves garlic, crushed with a dash of salt
1 tablespoon rice

Steps:

1. Fry onion with shortening until soft. Stir in spinach.
2. Place water in a pot. Add spinach mixture and spices.
3. Stir mixture occasionally until it boils. Add rice. Cook for 15 minutes.
4. Fry garlic and parsley with shortening for 5 minutes. Add to soup.
5. Add kibbi balls to soup. Cook for 5 minutes. Remove from heat. Serve hot.

Tomato Soup

Hisaa al tamatem

A well known soup in the Arab world.

Serves: 6
Preparation time: 30 minutes
Cooking time: 45 minutes

Ingredients:

400 g (14 oz) lean meat, minced
¹/₂ cup chopped parsley
¹/₂ cup broken vermicelli
¹/₂ kg (16 oz) soft red tomatoes, washed and squeezed
1 teaspoon salt
¹/₂ teaspoon ground allspice
2 tablespoons butter
4 cups water

Steps:

1. Mix the meat with half the amount of salt and allspice. Divide into small balls.
2. Fry the meat with shortening over medium heat for 5 minutes.
3. Add water, tomato juice, salt and allspice to meat and cook for ¹/₂ hour or till tender.
4. When it boils, add vermicelli, and simmer for 15 minutes. Add parsley and simmer for 1 minute.
5. Serve it hot.

Lentil Soup

Hisaa al adas

An Arabian hot appetizer.

Serves: 4
Preparation time: 20 minutes
Cooking time: 1 hour 40 minutes

Ingredients:

1 cup brown lentils
2 tablespoons rice
6 cups water
1/2 teaspoon salt
1/2 teaspoon ground cumin
1/4 teaspoon ground allspice
1 medium onion, finely chopped
1 tablespoon shortening or butter or vegetable oil
1/4 cup finely chopped fresh parsley
1 pitta, toasted and cut into cubes

Steps:

1. Wash lentils and rice well. Place in a pot with water. Bring to a boil. Cover and simmer gently for about 1½ hour.
2. Transfer the soup to a food processor or blender. Add 1 cup of water and blend well.
3. Put the mixture in the pot. Simmer over low heat. Add allspice, cumin and salt.
4. Fry the chopped onion till soft. Add to lentil mixture. Bring the mixture to a boil for 10 minutes. Add chopped parsley.
5. Serve soup with toasted bread and lemon wedges.

Sour Lentil Soup

Hisaa al adas bhamud

We advise you to prepare this soup in cold winter days. It is both easy and nutritious.

Serves: 4
Preparation time: 1 hour
Cooking time: 50 minutes

Ingredients:

1¹/₂ cups white lentils, picked stones, washed and
  drained
¹/₂ kg (16 oz) Swiss chard, trimmed and roughly chopped
1 head garlic, crushed with a dash of salt
¹/₂ cup finely chopped fresh coriander
¹/₂ cup oil or butter
¹/₂ cup lemon juice
4 cups water
1 teaspoon salt
3 medium potatoes, peeled and diced
¹/₄ cup finely chopped onions
1 teaspoon ground cumin

Steps:

1. Put lentils and water in a pot over high heat, bring to a boil. Lower heat, Simmer for 25 minutes.
2. Add Swiss chard and potatoes. Cook over low heat for 15 minutes.
3. Fry onions in oil, then add garlic and coriander, fry till fragrant for about 1 minute.
4. Add garlic mixture, cumin, and lemon juice to lentil mixture. Cook for 10 minutes.
5. Serve hot.

Chicken with Rice

Makloubat dajaj

A main meal of chicken and rice.

Serves: 4
Preparation time: 20 minutes
Cooking time: 1 hour

Ingredients:

1 chicken, about 1 ¹/₂ kg (48 oz)
2 cups long grain rice
400 g (14 oz) minced meat
¹/₄ cup fried pine nuts
¹/₂ cup fried almonds
2 medium sized onions (1 whole, 1 finely
   chopped)
¹/₄ cup vegetable oil and butter mixture
1 teaspoon ground cinnamon
2 teaspoons salt (as desired)
a dash of ground allspice
2 tablespoons butter
1 cup canned mushrooms (as desired)
1 cardamom pod, 1 nutmeg, 1 clove
2 cinnamon stalks

Steps:

1. Wash the chicken well and cut into 4 pieces.
2. Fry chicken pieces in oil and butter mixture until golden from both sides.
3. Put it in a deep, heavy pan and add to it one peeled onion with 1 teaspoon of salt, cardamom pod, clove, nutmeg and cinnamon sticks.
4. Add 1¹/₂ liters of water, cover and cook over medium heat for 30 minutes. Reserve stock.
5. Fry finely chopped onions in butter, keep stirring till soft and golden.
6. Add minced meat, allspice, cinnamon, and salt to chopped onions and fry for 10 minutes over medium heat.
7. Wash rice and drain, then add to meat and onion. Stir occasionally over low heat for 3 minutes.
8. Add 4 cups of boiling chicken stock to the rice, add mushrooms and cover. Cook rice over high heat for 5 minutes. Lower heat to low and cook for 20 minutes.
9. Pile rice onto large platter with chicken pieces in center and spread over the nuts. Serve hot with cucumber mixed with yoghurt and salad.

Rice with Fresh Broad Beans

Riz bfool akhdar

A main meal served usually with mixed green salad.

Serves: 5
Preparation time: 20 minutes
Cooking time: 45 minutes

Ingredients:

¹/₂ kg (16 oz) minced meat
¹/₂ kg (16 oz) green broad beans, trimmed
2 cups long grain rice
3 ¹/₂ cups water
3 medium onions, finely chopped
1 teaspoon salt
¹/₂ teaspoon ground cinnamon
2 tablespoons butter or shortening
¹/₂ cup fried pine nuts

Steps:

1. Fry onion with butter until soft. Add meat, salt and cinnamon. Cook until meat is brown and tender.
2. Add beans to meat mixture and cook for 5 minutes. Add water and cook over medium heat for 10 minutes.
3. Add rice to pot and bring to a boil for 5 minutes. Cover pot, lower heat, and continue cooking for another 20 minutes or until rice is tender.

Prawns and Rice

Riz bil kraydis

Another delicious Saudi Arabian main meal.

Serves: 5
Preparation time: 20 minutes
Cooking time: 45 minutes

Ingredients:

¹/₂ kg (16 oz) uncooked prawns, cleaned
2 cups long grain rice, washed and drained
¹/₄ cup frozen green peas
¹/₄ cup finely chopped carrots
1 teaspoon salt
¹/₄ teaspoon ground saffron
1 teaspoon grated green ginger or ¹/₄ teaspoon
  ground dried ginger
¹/₄ teaspoon ground piquant pepper
1 large onion, finely chopped
2 cloves garlic, crushed with a dash of salt
¹/₄ cup vegetable oil

Steps:

1. Fry prawns in oil for 5 minutes over high heat. Remove from heat and put on absorbent paper. Add all ingredients except rice to pot, stirring constantly for 2 minutes.
2. Add 1 liter water and bring to a boil for 10 minutes over moderate heat.
3. Add rice and see that water is covering mixture. If not, add some.
4. Cook for 15 minutes then lower heat, cook for another 10 minutes until rice is cooked. Stir in prawns until cooked.
5. Serve hot with sesame paste dip.

Rice with Truffles

Riz bil laham wa alkima

A hearty and satisfying dish for a cold winter day.

Serves: 5
Preparation time: 30 minutes
Cooking time: 2 $^1/_2$ hours

Ingredients:

1 kg (32 oz) truffles
1 small onion, finely chopped
3 cups long grain rice, washed and drained
400 g (14 oz) minced meat
600 g (20 oz) stew meat, diced
3 tablespoons shortening or butter
a dash of salt (as desired)
a dash of ground cinnamon
a dash of ground pepper
1 cup fried pine nuts and almonds (for garnishing)
1 litre (4 cups) water
1 tablespoon salt (for cleaning truffles)

Steps:

1. Soak truffles in cold water for 15 minutes. Peel using a sharp knife.
2. Put one litre of water and salt in a pot. Add truffles, bring to a boil. Chop into medium size pieces.
3. Sauté stew pieces with shortening until golden. Place aside.

4. Sauté stew meat with a dash of salt in the same shortening. Transfer meat to another pot. Add 2 litres of water to the pot and cook for 2 hours. Reserve stock.
5. Sauté onion with the same shortening on medium heat until transparent. Add minced meat, cinnamon, pepper, and salt to onion. Cook until meat is brown and tender.
6. Use 6 cups of stock to cook rice. Add rice to stock. Cover pot. Bring to a boil for 5 minutes. Reduce heat and cook for 20 minutes.
7. Spoon rice into a platter. Top with truffles, minced meat, and stew meat. Garnish with fried pine nuts and almonds.

Biryani Rice

Riz biryani

A Saudi classic, perfect for lunches, buffets, and suppers alike.

Serves: 5
Preparation time: 30 minutes
Cooking time: about 1 hour

Ingredients:

¹/₂ kg (16 oz) shoulder meat, cubed
2 cups long grain rice (Basmati), washed
³/₄ cup chopped onion
2 tablespoons shortening or butter
¹/₄ teaspoon saffron threads, soaked in ¹/₄ cup of water
1 teaspoon ground dried coriander
1 teaspoon ground cinnamon
1 teaspoon ground ginger
1 teaspoon cumin seeds
4 cups chicken stock
salt (as desired)
2 bay leaves
¹/₄ teaspoon ground clove
¹/₂ teaspoon ground nutmeg
¹/₂ cup finely chopped fresh coriander
2 tablespoons butter
¹/₂ cup fried onion rings, for garnish
60 g (2 oz) roasted cashew nuts
¹/₂ cup seeded raisins

Steps:

1. Heat shortening in a pot over low heat. Stir in onions until golden.
2. Stir in meat. Add coriander (dried and fresh), bay leaves, and spices (except saffron). Stir until meat becomes golden.
3. Remove bay leaves. Add salt, saffron, chicken stock, and rice to the same pot (stock level should be 5 cm higher than rice level). Add butter. Cover pot. Cook over low heat until tender (and the water evaporates).
4. Mix mixture with a spoon. To serve, line a large serving platter with rice-meat mixture, sprinkle fried onion rings, cashew nuts and sultanas. Serve hot

Rice with Vegetables

Riz maa khoudar

It is a side-dish, served with fish or meat.

Serves: 3

Preparation : 20 minutes

Cooking time: 45 minutes

Ingredients:

2 cups long grain rice
1 cup finely chopped carrots
1 cup frozen green peas
300 g (10 oz) minced meat
$^1/_2$ cup blanched and fried almonds
4 cups chicken or meat stock (or water)
2 tablespoons shortening (butter)
Salt (as desired)
a dash of cinnamon and pepper

Steps:

1. Place shortening in a pot over medium heat, fry minced meat with spices until tender, then add carrots till soft.
2. Add peas, salt and stock. Bring to a boil. Cook for 20 minutes.
3. Add rice and cover. Cook for 5 minutes. Reduce heat to low and cook for another 20 minutes.
4. Serve garnished with almonds.

Saudi Arabian Rice and Meat

Kapse

Kapsé, is a Saudi Arabian main meal.

Serves: 10
Preparation time: 45 minutes
Cooking time: 2 hours 30 minutes

Ingredients:

2 ¹/₂ kg (60 oz) lamb leg or shoulder meat, large
  cubes
4 cups long grain rice
¹/₂ kg (16 oz) carrots, peeled and finely chopped
1 green pepper, seeded and finely chopped
¹/₂ kg (16 oz) green peas
1 kg (32 oz) red tomatoes, peeled and chopped
1 kg (32 oz) finely chopped onion
1 medium sized garlic head, peeled and crushed
¹/₂ teaspoon ground saffron
¹/₄ teaspoon ground cardamom
¹/₂ teaspoon ground cinnamon
¹/₂ teaspoon ground allspice
¹/₄ teaspoon ground white pepper
1 tablespoon salt
shortening for frying
Fried almonds and pine nuts for garnishing

Steps:

1. Fry meat pieces till brown from both sides. Cover with water, bring to a boil then cook gently over medium heat for 2 hours or till tender. Reserve stock.
2. Soak rice for 15 minutes. Drain, wash well, then drain again.
3. Add shortening to a pot, fry on medium heat all ingredients except rice and meat. Cook on low heat for about 10 minutes, or until tender.
4. Add rice to vegetables in the pot, stir fry for 4 minutes on medium heat. Add stock meat until the stock covers the rice. Cover pot. Cook on low heat for 30 minutes or until tender.
5. Serve rice in a large platter. Garnish with meat, almonds, and pine nuts.

Sauce:

Ingredients:

2 cups meat stock
1 large onion, peeled and finely chopped
2 large tomatoes, peeled and finely chopped
2 cloves garlic, peeled and crushed
1 tablespoon tomato paste
$^1/_4$ cup chopped celery
1 teaspoon salt (as desired)
1 teaspoon cinnamon
2 tablespoons shortening

Steps:

1. Fry onion, garlic and tomato in shortening. Add tomato paste, salt, cinnamon and meat stock.
2. Cook mixture on medium heat. When it thickens, add celery.
3. Serve the sauce beside the Kapsé platter.

Overturned Eggplant

Makloubat al bathinjan

Casseroles are ideal for the cook who likes to entertain, because they usually demand a minimum of last-minute attention and can be assembled in advance.

Serves: 5
Preparation time: 15 minutes
Cooking time: 45 minutes

Ingredients:

2 cups long grain rice, washed and drained
1/2 kg (16 oz) minced meat
1 medium onion, peeled and finely chopped
1 kg (32 oz) medium round eggplants
2 tablespoons shortening or butter (for frying meat and onion)
4 cups vegetable oil (for frying eggplants)
1/2 cup fried pinenuts and almonds
1/4 teaspoon ground allspice
1/4 teaspoon ground cinnamon
1/4 teaspoon ground black pepper
4 cups water

Steps:

1. Peel eggplants. Chop lengthwise into 1 cm thick slices. Sprinkle some salt over eggplants and leave aside for 1 hour. Fry eggplants in oil, remove and drain on absorbant paper.
2. Sauté onion with shortening until transparent over medium heat. Stir in meat, salt, and spices. Cook until meat is brown and tender.
3. Arrange in layers in a pot: 1/4 quantity meat, eggplants, remaining meat and rice. Add gradually water.
4. Place pot over moderate heat. Boil for 5 minutes. Lower heat and cook for 20 minutes or until water evaporates. Turn over pot into a large plate (larger than pot).
5. Sprinkle fried pine nuts and fried almonds on top of the eggplants. Serve hot accompanied with yoghurt and salads.

Potato and Burghul Kibbi

Kibbi healeh

A new way of preparing kibbi from potato and burghul.

Serves: 5
Preparation time: 30 minutes
Cooking time: 45 minutes

Ingredients:

3 cups smooth burghul
2 medium potatoes
a dash of ground coriander
a dash of ground cumin
a bunch of fresh coriander, finely chopped
1 teaspoon salt
¹/₂ kg (16 oz) onion, peeled and sliced
1 tablespoon pomegranate thickened juice
a dash of ground turmeric
¹/₂ cup vegetable oil

Steps:

1. Boil potatoes until cooked. Peel and process using a manual processor. Soak burghul for 10 minutes. Wash and drain well.
2. Knead burghul with potatoes, salt, and half the quantity of spices (except turmeric) into a smooth dough.
3. Fry onion rings, salt, and remaining spices in some oil. Stir in turmeric and pomegranate juice on moderate heat until soft.
4. First way: Spread potato and burghul dough onto a baking tray like baked meat kibbi (p.114). Second way: Divide potato dough into egg sized balls. Smooth balls with wet palms. Make a hole in the middle with your forefinger. Work finger round in the hole until you have a shell of even thickness. Fry in hot oil until golden. Place on absorbent paper. When cool, fill with onion filling.
5. Serve accompanied with vegetable salad.

Grilled Wheat Grains

Freekeh

A delicious Syrian dish of grilled wheat grains with meat.

Serves: 5
Preparation time: about 45 minutes
Cooking time: 3 hours

Ingredients:

400 g (14 oz) lamb stew meat, cubed
2 cups freekeh (grilled green wheat)
1 medium sized onion, peeled
2 tablespoons shortening or butter
1 teaspoon salt
¹/₂ teaspoon ground cinnamon
¹/₂ cup pine nuts fried in vegetable oil
¹/₂ cup blanched and fried almonds
some fat

Steps:

1. Fry meat with 1 tablespoon shortening till brown all over.
2. Cover with water, add peeled onion, salt, cinnamon, cook over medium heat for 2 hours or till tender.
3. Remove meat, put aside. Reserve stock.
4. Remove stones from freekeh, wash and drain. Fry freekeh with fat and shortening.
5. Bring stock to a boil, adjust salt. Add freekeh and see that stock is about 7 cm above freekeh.
6. Bring to a boil over medium heat. Reduce heat and cook for 30 minutes (don't stir mixture).
7. Serve it garnished with meat, almonds and pine nuts.

Strained Lentils

Mjadra msaffaye

A meatless dish. It is both nutritious and filling.

Serves: 4
Preparation time: 30 minutes
Cooking time: 2 hours

Ingredients:

1 ¹/₂ cups brown lentils, picked stones, washed, drained
¹/₂ cup rice, soaked for 1 hour
¹/₂ cup vegetable oil
¹/₂ cup finely chopped onion
1 teaspoon salt

Steps:

1. Put lentils in a pot, cover with water, bring to a boil over high heat. Cover. Simmer for 1 hour and 30 minutes till cooked.
2. Process with liquid into a purée.
3. Put lentil purée in a pot, add rice, salt and 1 cup water. Cover. Cook over medium heat for 10 minutes.
4. Fry onions. Add to lentil mixture. Lower heat. Cook for 15 minutes till rice is tender.
5. Pour in serving bowls. Serve cold with salads.

Lima Bean Stew

Yakhnet al fasoulia

When you have a yearning for grandma's real home cooking, try this recipe.

Serves: 5
Preparation time: 20 minutes
Cooking time: 2 hours 40 minutes

Ingredients:

$1/2$ kg (16 oz) dried or fresh lima beans, soaked in water for one night
400 g (14 oz) stewing meat, cubed
2 cups tomato juice
3 tablespoons shortening or butter
1 tablespoon salt
a dash of ground allspice
6 cloves garlic, crushed with $1/2$ cup finely chopped coriander

Steps:

1. Fry meat with 1 tablespoon of shortening until golden-brown. Put meat in a generous quantity of water in a pot. Cook over medium heat for 2 hours.
2. Cook beans in double its amount of salted water. Remove and drain.
3. Fry beans in the remaining shortening for 3 minutes. Add meat, meat's stock, tomato juice, salt, and allspice. Cover and cook for 30 minutes (add water if necessary).
4. Fry coriander and garlic till fragrant for 2 minutes. Add to beans mixture. Cook for 1 minute.
5. Serve beans hot, accompanied with cooked rice.

Lentils with Dough

Harra isbau bil-ajeen

A very delicious Syrian appetizer.

Serves: 5
Preparation time: 1 hour
Cooking time: 1 hour 30 minutes

Ingredients:

1 ¹/₂ cups brown lentils
8 cups water
1 ¹/₂ cups all purpose flour
2 large onions, chopped (¹/₂ cup)
1 cup finely chopped fresh coriander
¹/₂ cup lemon juice
1 cup olive oil
2 tablespoons pomegranate thickened juice
1 head garlic, crushed with a dash of salt
¹/₂ cup vegetable oil
¹/₂ teaspoon of salt
a dash of ground allspice

Dough Steps:

1. Put flour with ¹/₂ cup of water and some salt in a bowl. Knead dough and leave for 2 hours then sprinkle flour over it.
2. Roll out the dough on a floured surface, till it becomes as thin as possible and round shaped. Fold about 7 cm at one end. Sprinkle flour and fold another 7 cm, same side. Repeat until dough is all layers.
3. Cut dough into small squares then open them. Put half the quantity in a flat dish. Fry the other half in ¹/₄ cup of hot vegetable oil until golden. Use to garnish at the end.

Steps:

1. Pick small stones or dirt from lentils then wash lentils well, and place in a heavy pan with water. Bring to a boil. Cook on medium heat for 1 ¹/₂ hours or until tender. Add lemon juice, pomegranate juice, olive oil, salt, and pepper. Mix well.
2. Fry sliced onions with ¹/₄ cup of vegetable oil until golden. Add half the quantity of onions to the lentils.
3. Fry in vegetable oil crushed garlic, coriander and add half the quantity to the lentils.
4. Add unfried dough squares to lentil mixture. Keep stirring till dough is cooked (about 20 minutes).
5. Serve hot or cold, garnished with fried onions, coriander and fried dough pieces.

Lentils with Rice

Mdardra

An Arabian meatless meal.

Serves: 5
Preparation time: 15 minutes
Cooking time: 1 hour

Ingredients:

1 cup white lentils
2 cups long grain rice
4 medium onions, peeled and sliced lengthwise,
  fried
¹/₄ cup vegetable oil
1 teaspoon salt
4 cups water

Steps:

1. Remove stones and dirt from lentils then wash.
2. Put water in a pot. Add lentils. Bring to a boil over medium heat, then reduce heat and cook for 25 minutes or till tender with pot covered.
3. Add rice and salt, if water isn't double the quantity of rice and lentils, add more water.
4. Cover and boil over low heat for 30 minutes.
5. Garnish with onions and serve with yoghurt-cucumber salad.

Artichoke with Meat

Ardi chawki bil lahem

A very tasty dish perfect for all occasions.

Serves: 6
Preparation time: 30 minutes
Cooking time: 1 hour 15 minutes

Ingredients:

12 artichoke heads
400 g (14 oz) minced meat
1 medium onion, finely chopped
1/2 cup fried pine nuts
2 tablespoons butter for frying meat and onion
1/2 teaspoon salt
1/4 cup lemon juice
1 cup finely chopped boiled carrots (optional)
a dash of ground pepper
a dash of ground allspice
a dash of flour
2 cups water for cooking artichokes

Steps:

1. Cover artichoke heads with water, flour and lemon juice. Boil for 10 minutes. Remove and fry in some butter. Place aside.
2. Fry onion until soft. Stir in meat, salt, and spice. Cook on low heat for 15 minutes, stirring occasionally.
3. Remove meat from heat. Stir in carrots.
4. Distribute meat mixture over prepared artichokes. Place in a tray. Add water. Cover and cook over moderate heat for 15 minutes or until tender.
5. Serve artichokes hot, garnished with pine nuts and accompanied by cooked rice, radishes and lemon.

Stuffed Gourds and Eggplants

Kareh wa bathinjan mahshowan

A main meal, served with green onions and fresh mint. You can follow the same recipe and substitute gourds and eggplants for baby marrow.

Serves: 4

Preparation time: about 1 hour

Cooking time: about 2 hours

Ingredients:

750 g (24 oz) small gourds (if small is unavailable cut the large into 4 pieces crosswise)
750g (24 oz) purple black, long eggplants
$^1/_2$ cup short grain rice
500 g (16 oz) minced meat
1 head garlic, peeled and crushed with a dash of salt
$^1/_2$ kg (16 oz) tomatoes, peeled and finely chopped
$^1/_2$ teaspoon ground dried mint
1 tablespoon lemon juice
a dash of ground black pepper and ground cinnamon
1 tablespoon shortening or vegetable oil
$^1/_2$ tablespoon salt (as desired)
$^1/_4$ cup finely chopped onion

Steps:

1. Peel gourds.
2. Roll eggplants on a smooth surface.
3. Remove stems.
4. Core with a special corer, wash and drain.
5. Filling: Mix meat, onion, rice and season well.
6. Stuff eggplants and gourds. Don't overstuff.
7. Arrange in a pot. Sprinkle salt. Add tomatoes, garlic, mint, lemon juice, shortening and water to cover. Cook over high heat. Bring to a boil.
8. Reduce heat. Cook till tender for about 2 hours. Serve hot.

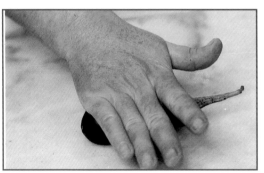

Stuffed Zucchini with Yoghurt

Kousa mahshu bil laban

A main meal for those who like yoghurt.

Serves: 5
Preparation time: 1 hour
Cooking time: 50 minutes

Ingredients:

2 kg (64 oz) zucchini, medium size
1 ¹/₂ kg (46 oz) yoghurt
3 cloves garlic, crushed with a dash of salt
leaves of 5 mint stalks, finely chopped
4 cups water
¹/₂ teaspoon salt (as desired)

Filling:
¹/₂ kg (16 oz) ground meat
1 ¹/₂ cups rice
2 tablespoons shortening or butter
a dash of salt
¹/₄ teaspoon ground cinnamon
¹/₄ cup fried pine nuts (optional)

Steps:

1. Cook yoghurt (see p 9).
2. Wash zucchini, cut off stem and hollow them with an apple corer.
3. Mix all ingredients of filling.
4. Stuff zucchini. Put in a pot with water, salt, and ¹/₄ the quantity of cooked yoghurt. Cook over medium heat for 30 minutes.
5. Add zucchini to boiling yoghurt, cook over medium heat for 15 minutes. Add crushed garlic with dried mint to mixture. Boil for another 5 minutes.
6. Serve with spring onions and fresh mint.

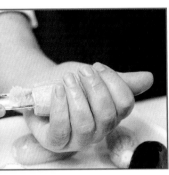

Green Bean Stew

Yakhnet lubya

A famous stew, usually served with cooked rice and tomato-onion salad seasoned with lemon juice, crushed garlic and olive oil.

Serves: 4
Preparation time: about 35 minutes
Cooking time: about 45 minutes

Ingredients:

1 kg (32 oz) green beans, string, snip off the ends, snip each into two, wash and drain
750 g (24 oz) stew lamb cutlets
1/2 teaspoon ground pepper
2 tablespoons shortening or butter
1 teaspoon salt
3 cups water

Steps:

1. Fry meat with shortening over medium heat till brown. Season.
2. Stir in green beans for 15 minutes on low heat.
3. Add water, salt and pepper. Cover and cook on medium heat until boiling.
4. Lower heat. Continue cooking until beans are tender. Serve hot accompanied by cooked rice.

Stuffed Zucchini in Tomato Sauce

Kousa mahshou bil-tamatem

A famous dish in the Arab world.

Serves: 5
Preparation time: about 40 minutes
Cooking time: 1 hour

Ingredients:

1 kg (32 oz) medium zucchini
200 g (7 oz) minced meat
1 cup short grain rice, washed
1 kg (32 oz) red tomatoes, peeled and chopped
2 teaspoons salt
*a dash of ground allspice and black pepper (as
  desired)*
a dash of ground cinnamon (as desired)
1 tablespoon shortening or butter
5 cloves garlic, crushed with a dash of salt
2 cups water
4 tablespoons lemon juice

Steps:

1. Wash well zucchini. Remove stems using a knife. Hollow out using an apple corer. Wash zucchini inside and out. Drain.
2. Filling: Mix minced meat with rice. Stir in salt and spices.
3. Stuff zucchini, shake each after filling it so that the filling is well distributed (don't over stuff). Arrange in a pot. Invert a plate on top.
4. Strain tomatoes using a colander. Add 2 cups of water, shortening, and a dash of salt. Place tomato juice in a pot over medium heat. When it boils, add to zucchini. Cook for 1 hour, or until tender. Add crushed garlic and lemon juice. Cook for 5 minutes.
5. Serve zucchini and sauce hot separately or together in a large bowl.

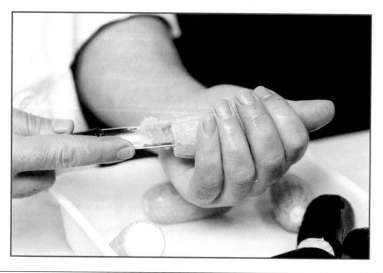

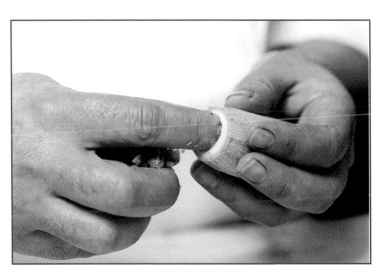

Eggplant Stew

Yakhnet bathinjan

As you notice, onion is an essential ingredient in the Arabian kitchen. This dish gets its special taste from it.

Serves: 4

Preparation time: about 1 hour

Cooking time: about 2 hours

Ingredients:

500 g (16 oz) black eggplants, peeled, cubed
600 g (20 oz) lamb stew meat, cubed
1 cup finely chopped onion
1 tablespoon salt
a dash of ground black pepper and allspice
vegetable oil
1 tablespoon butter or shortening

Steps:

1. Sprinkle salt on eggplant cubes. Place aside for 1 hour.
2. Fry eggplant cubes in hot oil. Remove and drain on absorbent paper.
3. Fry chopped onion for 2 minutes then sauté meat with 2 tablespoons of butter. Cover with water, add salt and spices, and cook on high heat. Bring to a boil. Cover pot and cook on medium heat for 2 hours.
4. Add fried eggplants to meat and stock. Cover pot and cook for 10 minutes.
5. Serve eggplant stew with lemon wedges and eggplant dip.

Lebanese Jew's Mallow

Serves: 5
Preparation time: 1 hour
Cooking time: 3 hours

Ingredients:

¹/₂ kg (16 oz) of fresh Jew's mallow (melokhia) leaves
1 kg (32 oz) chicken, cleaned quartered
600 g (20 oz) lamb stew meat, cubed
1 large onion, peeled
1 cup fresh coriander, finely chopped
3 heads garlic, peeled
¹/₄ cup ground dried coriander
1 tablespoon salt (as desired)
3 tablespoons shortening or butter
3 tablespoons shortening or butter (for frying jew's mallow)
a dash of ground white pepper, cinnamon, and black pepper

Steps:

1. Fry meat with 2 tablespoons of shortening and a dash of salt, cinnamon, and black pepper. Remove and place in another pot. Cover with water and cook over moderate heat. Bring to a boil then lower heat, cover pot, and continue cooking for 2 hours until tender.
2. Fry chicken with same shortening and a dash of salt and white pepper on low heat. Cover with water. Cover pot and cook on moderate heat for 45 minutes. Remove and put aside.
3. Grill onion. Process onion with dried coriander, one peeled head of garlic, and a dash of salt. Put aside.
4. Fry jew's mallow in batches with shortening. Remove and place aside.
5. Fry remaining garlic and onion mixture with remaining shortening. Stir in coriander and jew's mallow leaves. Add meat and stock.
6. Cover pot and cook over low heat for 1 hour until tender.
7. Serve hot garnished with chicken and a dash of cinnamon accompanied by cooked rice, radishes, and lemon.

Spinach Stew
Yakhnet sabanegh

One of the many Arabian stews.

Serves: 4
Preparation time: 40 minutes
Cooking time: 20 minutes

Ingredients:

1 kg (32 oz) spinach, washed, stalks removed,
*   roughly chopped*
¹/₄ kg (8 oz) lean lamb or beef, minced or cubed
2 medium onions, chopped
2 tablespoons shortening or butter
1 tablespoon salt (as desired)
a dash of ground allspice
¹/₄ cup fried pine nuts
4 cloves garlic, peeled and crushed with a dash of
*   salt*
¹/₂ cup finely chopped fresh coriander
1 liter water

Steps:

1. Boil water in a pot. Add bicarbonate of sodium then chopped spinach. Bring to a boil for 3 minutes. Remove and wash well. Drain. Put aside.
2. Sauté onion with shortening or butter over moderate heat until transparent. Stir in meat, salt and allspice until tender.
3. Stir in garlic then add coriander and spinach. Mix well. Add 1 cup of water. Cook over moderate heat for 20 minutes or until tender.
4. Garnish with pine nuts. Serve accompanied with cooked rice.

Pea with Carrots Stew

Yakhnit al bazila maa al jazar

Through out the world peas are cooked in different ways. This is one of the good stew recipes.

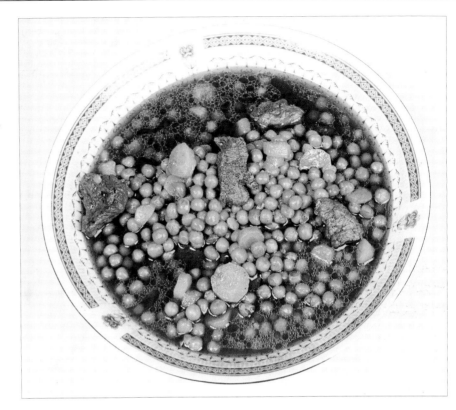

Serves: 4

Preparation time: 20 minutes

Cooking time: 2 hours 20 minutes

Ingredients:

1 kg (32 oz) green peas (frozen)
1/2 kg (16 oz) lamb or beef stew meat, cubed
1/2 kg (16 oz) carrots, peeled and chopped
1 teaspoon salt (as desired)
a dash of ground allspice
a dash of ground cinnamon
1 1/2 tablespoons tomato paste
4 cups of water
3 tablespoons shortening or butter

Steps:

1. Fry meat with 1¹/₂ tablespoons butter until golden. Add spices and water. Cover pot and cook for 2 hours until tender.
2. Fry carrots in remaining butter for 3 minutes on low heat. Stir in peas then tomato paste.
3. Add meat to peas. Cover with stock. Cover pot. Cook on low heat for 20 minutes.
4. Serve hot with cooked rice.

Note: You can substitute tomato paste with garlic and coriander mixture.

Cabbage Leaves Stuffed with Meat

Warak al malfouf al mahshou bil lahem

A nutritious main dish.

Serves: 4
Preparation time: 40 minutes
Cooking time: 2 hours

Ingredients:

1 ¹/₂ kg (48 oz) cabbage
1 cup short grain rice
400 g (14 oz) minced meat
¹/₄ cup lemon juice (as desired)
¹/₄ cup shortening or butter
¹/₄ cup Seville orange juice
1 teaspoon salt
a dash of ground paprika
a dash of ground cinnamon
a dash of ground cumin
3 cups water
1 medium head crushed garlic
¹/₂ teaspoon dried mint (as desired)
1 tablespoon pomegranate thickened juice

Steps:

1. Peel off cabbage leaves. Blanch some leaves in boiling water for few minutes. Remove with a slotted spoon and put in cold water then put in a colander. Repeat same procedure with remaining leaves.
2. Mix rice with minced meat, spices and salt.
3. Place cabbage leaf, shiny side down, on a work surface. Cut into 2 or 3 pieces (depending on size of leaf).
4. Place crosswise about a tablespoon of stuffing (depending on the size of leaf), and fold ends.
5. Roll firmly and repeat procedure with remaining leaves.
6. Place ¹/₂ cup of butter in a pot. Pack leaf rolls close together in layers. Invert a heavy plate on top to keep rolls in shape during cooking.
7. Add to pot lemon juice, Seville orange juice, 3 cups of water, pomegranate juice, garlic, dry mint, and a dash of salt. Bring to a boil on moderate heat. Cover pot. Cook on low heat for 2 hours or until tender (add water if evaporated).
8. Serve hot accompanied by radishes.

Note: you can add some stuffed zucchini.

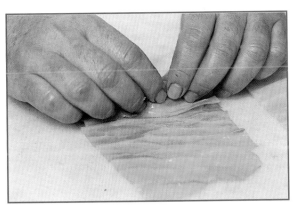

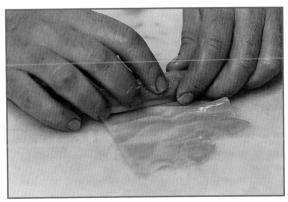

Stuffed Vine Leaves and Zucchini

Warak inab wa kousa mahshuwan

A famous main meal, perfect for a special occasion. Make extra and have them for lunch the next day.

Serves: 8

Preparation time: 1 hour

Cooking time: 2 hours

Ingredients:

1 kg (32 oz) lamb cutlets, fried with shortening or butter
¹/₂ kg (16 oz) vine leaves, trimmed
1 kg (32 oz) small zucchini
750 g (24 oz) ground meat
1 ¹/₄ cups rice
¹/₄ teaspoon ground black pepper
1 cup lemon juice
1 head garlic, peeled
1 teaspoon salt (as desired)

Steps:

1. Trim vine leaves. Wash.
2. Pour water in a pot. Bring to a boil.
3. Dip vine leaves in boiling water and lift immediately. Place in cold water then drain.
4. Prepare stuffing by mixing: rice, ground meat, salt and pepper.
5. Spread each vine leaf, shiny side down on a work surface. Put 1 tablespoon / or teaspoon (depending on size of leaf) stuffing on each leaf.
6. Fold sides and roll up into a small and neat roll.
7. Repeat with remaining ingredients.
8. Arrange cutlets in the pot, pack vine leaf rolls close together in layers with garlic cloves in between.

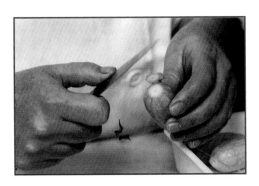

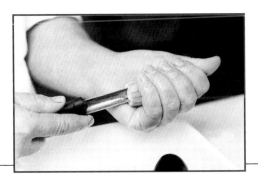

9. Invert a heavy plate on top to keep rolls in shape during cooking.
10. Wash zucchini and cut the stems.
11. Hollow zucchini using an apple corer. Wash from inside and out.
12. Stuff zucchini, not over filling them. Arrange zucchini on top of plate.
13. Add hot water to cover and lemon juice. Bring to a boil.
14. Cover and simmer gently over low heat for 2 hours or until leaves are tender (when cooking add some hot water if necessary to have stock left when served).
15. Arrange in a platter and serve with fresh mint and green onions.

Note: You can prepare steps 1-12 the day before cooking. Place in refrigerator for the next day.

Stuffed Pigeons
Al Hamam al mahshu

Egyptians are known for their delicious pigeon recipes. Try this recipe.

Serves: 4
Preparation time: 30 minutes
Cooking time: 1 hour

Ingredients:

8 pigeons, cleaned
200 g (7 oz) ground meat
$^1/_2$ cup rice
$^1/_4$ cup fried pine nuts
$^1/_2$ cup blanched and fried almonds
$^1/_4$ cup blanched and fried pistachio nuts
1 large onion, sliced into rings
$^1/_4$ teaspoon ground cinnamon
1 tablespoon shortening
butter
1 tablespoon salt (as desired)
$^1/_4$ teaspoon ground black pepper
2 bay leaves
4 cardamom pods

Steps:

1. Rub pigeons inside and out with $^1/_2$ quantity of salt and ground spices.
2. Fry meat in shortening. Add $^1/_4$ teaspoon salt and remaining ground spices. Mix for 5 minutes. Add $^1/_2$ cup of water.
3. Add rice to meat. Stir once. Cook on low heat until the water evaporates and the rice is half cooked.
4. Mix rice and meat with pistachio nuts, almonds, and pine nuts. Stuff pigeons (don't over-stuff). Stitch opening.
5. Place pigeons in a pot. Add bay leaves, cardamom pods, onion, and 2 cups of water. Cook over medium heat for 5 minutes. Remove scum as it appears. Add salt. Cover pot. Cook on low heat for 45 minutes.
6. Remove pigeons from stock. Brush with butter. Place in a hot oven (220°C/450°F) for 15 minutes until golden.
7. Arrange in platter. Serve hot.

Stuffed Chicken

Al Dajaj al mahshu

A main meal good for special occasions.

Serves: 4

Preparation time: 1 hour 15 minutes

Cooking time: nearly 1 hour

Ingredients:

1 kg (32 oz) chicken, cleaned
$^{1}/_{4}$ cup pine nuts, fried
$^{1}/_{4}$ cup blanched almonds, fried
$^{1}/_{4}$ cup blanched pistachio nuts, fried
200 g (7 oz) minced meat
$^{1}/_{4}$ cup shortening or butter
butter
$^{1}/_{4}$ teaspoon of: ground allspice, ground cinnamon and ground cardamon
1 tablespoon salt
$^{3}/_{4}$ cup long grain rice, washed
1 bay leaf

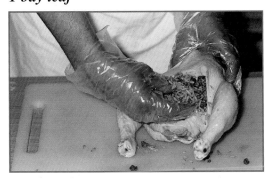

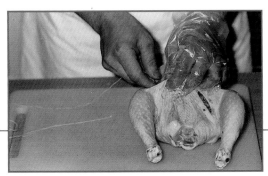

Steps:

1. Put the minced meat with shortening in the cooking pot, add $^{1}/_{4}$ teaspoon of salt and $^{1}/_{2}$ the quantity of the spices. Stir the mixture for 5 minutes, add 1 cup of water.
2. Add the rice to the meat and stir once. Leave it over moderate heat for 15 minutes.
3. Rub the chicken with the remaining spices inside and out.
4. Filling: Mix the cooked rice with pine nuts, almonds and pistachio nuts. Stuff the chicken with the mixture and stitch the opening.
5. Put the chicken on its back in a pot, add the bay leaf and cover with water. Leave over moderate heat, bring to a boil and add a dash of salt. Cover the pot and simmer for 40 minutes (remove scum as it appears).
6. Rub chicken with butter, put in an oven tray on high heat for 15 minutes, till brown and cooked.
7. Serve the chicken with bread and garnished with parsley.

Pigeons with Cracked Wheat

Hamam bil-fireek

We chose for you one of the best Saudi Arabian recipes. It is a national dish: delicious and nutritious.

Serves: 4
Preparation time: 35 minutes
Cooking time: 1 hour 25 minutes

Ingredients:

4 pigeons, cleaned
1 tablespoon ground cinnamon
¹/₂ cup butter
2 cups fireek (grilled green wheat), washed and drained
1 teaspoon ground black pepper (as desired)
¹/₄ cup finely chopped onion
¹/₃ cup fat
¹/₂ tablespoon ground cardamon
1 ¹/₂ tablespoons salt (as desired)
3 cups water
¹/₂ cup fried pine nuts
4 tablespoons flour

Steps:

1. Melt some fat with half the quantity of butter in a pan on medium heat. Fry onion in the butter mixture until soft. Stir in fireek for 5 minutes on low heat. Add water and spices. After 15 minutes, remove half the quantity of fireek. Place aside. Cook the remaining half for another 15 minutes or until water evaporates.
2. Rub pigeons with flour and some spices. Stuff pigeons with half the quantity of fireek. Stitch opening. Place pigeons in a pot. Cover with water. Bring to a boil. Lower heat. Cover pot and cook for 40 minutes.
3. Remove pigeons and drain from stock. Place on an oven tray. Brush pigeons with butter. Place tray in moderate heat oven (180°C/350°F). Cook for 20 minutes until pigeons are golden-brown.
4. Serve the remaining fireek in a platter. Place pigeons over fireek. Garnish with pine nuts.

Stuffed Boned Chicken

Dajaj mosahab mahshou

A delicious dish for boned and stuffed chicken breasts lovers.

Serves: 4
Preparation time: about 1 hour
Cooking time: about 1 hour

Ingredients:

4 boned chicken breasts (keep the bone on the wing for garnishing)
³/₄ cup long grain rice
300 g (10 oz) minced meat
2 tablespoons fried pine nuts
3 tablespoons fried pistachio nuts
¹/₂ cup shortening (or butter)
¹/₃ cup frozen peas
¹/₂ teaspoon of each: salt, ground cinnamon, all-spice, saffron, cardamom

Steps:

1. Rub chicken from inside and out with ¹/₂ quantity of spices.
2. Fry minced meat with shortening until tender. Stir in for 5 minutes peas, salt, and the remaining spices. Add 2 cups of water. Mix well.
3. Add rice to meat mixture. Cook on low heat for 25 minutes. Put aside.
4. Add pistachio and pine nuts to rice. Mix well. Stuff breasts with rice mixture. Stitch the opening.
5. Rub stuffed breasts with butter. Place stuffed breasts in a high heat oven (220°C/450°F) for 45 minutes or until golden and tender.
6. Serve stuffed breasts garnished with almonds accompanied by vegetable salad.

Barbecued Boned Chicken

Shish tawook

Children love them at lunches and dinners.

Serves: 4
Preparation time: 30 minutes
Cooking time: 30 minutes

Ingredients:

1 kg (32 oz) boned chicken
1 tablespoon ketchup
1 tablespoon tomato paste
1 teaspoon salt
$^1/_4$ teaspoon ground white pepper
a dash of ground ginger
5 cloves garlic, crushed
$^3/_4$ cup lemon juice
$^1/_2$ cup vegetable oil

Steps:

1. Mix all ingredients above. Soak for 24 hours in the refrigerator.
2. Place in an oven tray. Place tray in a (220°C/450°F) oven for 30 minutes. Lower heat, cook for 30 minutes or until tender (or thread chicken pieces onto skewers, alternate with mushrooms if desired).
3. Serve accompanied with french fries and garlic purée.

Chicken Shawarma

Shawarma al dajaj

A new way of preparing shawarma.

Serves: 8
Preparation time: 30 minutes
Cooking time: 45 minutes
Soaking time: 24 hours

Ingredients:

2 kg (64 oz) boned chicken, cut into finger size
   slices
2 cups lemon juice
1 ¹/₂ cups vegetable oil
a dash of salt (as desired)
a dash of ground white pepper
a dash of ground paprika
a dash of ground mastic
1 tablespoon ground 7 spices

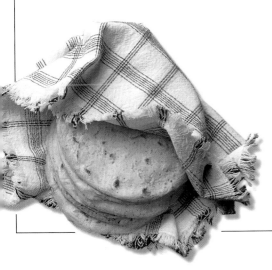

Steps:

1. Mix all ingredients above. Soak placed in the refrigerator for 24 hours.
2. Place in an oven tray. Enter the tray into a (220°C/450°F) oven for 45 minutes.
3. Serve accompanied with grilled tomatoes, french fries, and salads.

Chicken with Vegetables

Al dajaj maa al khoudar

A world wide known and loved dish.

Serves: 4
Preparation time: 30 minutes
Cooking time: about 1 hour

Ingredients:

1 chicken cleaned and cut into 4 pieces
$1/2$ kg (16 oz.) carrots, cooked and cut into circles
$1/2$ kg (16 oz.) zucchini, cooked and cut into slices (lengthwise)
$1/2$ cup canned mushrooms
$1/4$ cup cooked green peas
1 large onion, sliced
5 cloves garlic, crushed
$1/4$ cup vegetable oil and butter mixture
$1/4$ cup butter
$1/2$ cup lemon juice
4 cups water
$1/2$ tablespoon salt
$1/2$ teaspoon ground allspice
2 bay leaves
some chopped thyme leaves

Steps:

1. Fry chicken pieces with oil and butter until golden. Remove and place aside.
2. Fry garlic in half the quantity of butter. Add lemon juice, salt, allspice, water, bay leaves, and thyme. Bring to a boil on medium heat.
3. Add chicken pieces. Cook on low heat for 45 minutes. Remove and place on a large platter (reserve 2 cups of chicken stock to make chicken sauce).
4. Fry cooked vegetables in the remaining butter. Garnish chicken with vegetables. Serve hot accompanied with chicken sauce.

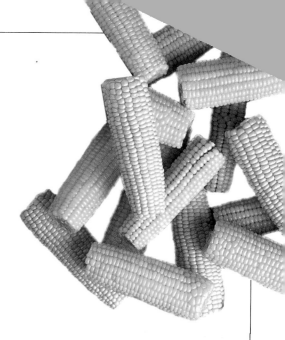

Chicken Sauce:

Ingredients:

2 cups chicken stock
1 medium onion
3 cloves garlic
1 carrot, peeled and
    chopped (into circles)
2 bay leaves

1 tablespoon cornflour
2 chopped celery stalks
$^1/_4$ cup chopped leek
1 tablespoon butter
a dash of salt
a dash of ground white pepper
2 cinnamon sticks

Steps:

1. Place all ingredients (except cornflour and butter) in a pot. Cook on moderate heat for 20 minutes. Remove bay leaves and cinnamon sticks.
2. Remove stock mixture from heat. Process. Return to pot.
3. Dissolve cornflour in some water. Add to processed mixture. Cook on low heat. Stir constantly until it boils.
4. Add butter (as desired), cook sauce until it thickens.

...en With ...onds

ajaj bil loz

A delicious Moroccan dish.

Serves: 5
Preparation time: 30 minutes
Cooking time: 60 minutes

Ingredients:

5 boneless, chicken breasts
1 cup fried almonds
¹/₄ cup chopped mushrooms, canned
¹/₄ cup finely chopped celery
1 ¹/₂ cups grated mozzarella cheese
1 cup milk
1 tablespoon flour
1 teaspoon salt
¹/₄ cup butter

Steps:

1. Melt butter in a pot. Add flour then milk.
2. Mix mushrooms with celery, salt, grated cheese, and almonds. Add mushroom mixture to flour mixture. Mix well.
3. Stuff each chicken piece with 1 tablespoon or more of stuffing. Stitch well.
4. Brush each piece with some butter. Arrange in a greased oven tray. Place in a moderate heat oven (180°C/350°F) for 1 hour or until tender.
5. Serve hot accompanied with chicken sauce (p. 97), boiled vegetables and cooked rice.

Fried Sparrows

Al asafir al mouhammara

Small birds are very tasty specially when cooked the right way. This is one of the good recipes.

Serves: 4
Preparation time: 20 minutes
Cooking time: 30 minutes

Ingredients:

8 sparrows, cleaned/or any game birds
$^1/_2$ teaspoon salt
$^1/_4$ cup lemon juice
1 tablespoon pomegranate thickened juice
1 tablespoon butter
a dash of white pepper

Steps:

1. Fry sparrows in butter over medium heat till golden brown on all sides. Season and cook over low heat for 25 minutes, stirring occasionally.
2. Add lemon juice and pomegranate juice and cook for another 10 minutes, stirring occasionally.
3. Serve hot with fried mushrooms and potatoes.

Palestinian Msakhan Chicken

sakhan al dajaj

The best Palestinian recipe. It is known all over the Arab world because it is very delicious.

Serves: 4
Preparation time: 30 minutes
Cooking time: 1 hour

Ingredients:

1 chicken (about 1 kg/32 oz),
*   cleaned and boned*
1 teaspoon salt (as desired)
$^1/_2$ teaspoon ground black pepper
a dash of olive oil
$^1/_2$ cup of vegetable oil and butter
*   mixture*
$^3/_4$ cup roughly chopped onion
3 tablespoons ground sumac
1 large pitta (30 cm diameter),
*   opened (makes 2 pieces)*

Steps:

1. Rub cleaned chicken inside and out with salt and pepper. Fry in hot oil and butter over medium heat, turn on all sides to brown. Place in a plate.
2. Fry onions in remaining oil mixture. Add sumac, stirring for 2 minutes. Add olive oil and remove mixture. Place 1 pitta piece in a tray, spread in the middle $^1/_2$ quantity of onion mixture, put chicken over onion mixture. Top with remaining onions, cover with the second pitta

piece (face inside part of bread downward). Sprinkle some water on bread.
3. Bake in a moderate heat oven (180°C/350°F) till tender (if pitta starts to burn, cover with aluminum foil).
4. Serve hot with its bread. Cut into several pieces.

Golden Chicken Wings

Jawaneh mohamara

You can serve this dish as an appetizer or a light meal.

Serves: 5 as an appetizer
Preparation time: 10 minutes
Cooking time: 30 minutes

Ingredients:

1 kg (32 oz) chicken wings, cleaned
2 cloves garlic, peeled, crushed with a teaspoon
  of salt
1 cup fresh coriander, finely chopped (as desired)
¹/₄ cup lemon juice
2 tablespoons shortening or butter
a dash of white pepper
1 medium onion, finely chopped

Steps:

1. Pass wings over gas fumes to get rid of remaining feathers.
2. Wash wings with soap and water. Drain using a colander.
3. Fry onion with shortening on medium heat till soft. Stir in garlic for 2 minutes.
4. Add wings rubbed with white pepper. Fry wings until golden.
5. Add lemon juice and stir for 1 minute. Stir in coriander. Remove from heat.
6. Serve wings hot accompanied with french fries.

Golden Chicken with Potatoes

Mohamar al batata bil dajaj

A delicious Jordanian dish. It consists of chicken with golden potatoes, coriander, and garlic.

Serves: 4

Preparation time: 20 minutes

Cooking time: 1 hour

Ingredients:

1 kg (32 oz) chicken, cleaned and cut into 4 pieces

1 kg (32 oz) potatoes, peeled and cubed

¹/₂ cup lemon juice

1 medium garlic head, crushed with a dash of salt

¹/₄ cup finely chopped coriander

¹/₄ cup vegetable oil

¹/₄ cup sliced onion

¹/₂ teaspoon ground allspice (as desired)

1 teaspoon salt (as desired)

¹/₂ teaspoon ground cinnamon

¹/₄ teaspoon ground cardamom

Steps:

1. Place chicken pieces in a pot. Cover with water. Add onion, allspice, salt, cinnamon, and cardamom. Cover pot and cook on medium heat for 40 minutes.
2. Remove chicken pieces from pot. Strain stock. Return chicken and stock to pot.
3. Fry potatoes in hot oil until golden. Remove and add to chicken and stock. Bring to a boil for 5 minutes.
4. Fry coriander and garlic in hot oil. Remove and add to chicken in pot. Mix mixture. Remove chicken from pot.
5. Serve hot in a platter. Squeeze over lemon juice.

Kibbi Balls with Shawarma

Akras al Kibbeh bil shawarma

A new exotic dish perfect for parties.

Serves: 7
Preparation time: 1 hour 30 minutes
Cooking time: 30 minutes

Ingredients:

1 kg (32 oz) finely ground lean meat
1 kg (32 oz) ground burghul (cracked wheat),
washed and drained
1 teaspoon salt
1 cup iced water
1/2 teaspoon ground cinnamon
1/2 teaspoon ground black pepper
6 cups vegetable oil
1 large peeled onion

Shawarma filling:
1 kg (32 oz) fillets cut into strips (7 cm length, 3
cm thickness)
200 g (7 oz) finely minced fat
2 large onions, peeled and sliced
1/4 cup vegetable oil
1/2 cup vinegar
1/2 tablespoon salt (as desired)
1 tablespoon ground 7 spices for Shawarma
(Lebanese spice)
a dash of ground mastic
1 teaspoon ground nutmeg
1 teaspoon cardamom pods

Steps:

1. Prepare large Kibbi balls (15 cm long) without preparing the filling (see p.104). Fry them without filling.
2. Prepare shawarma (see p. 108).
3. Slit kibbeh balls lengthwise on one side, fill with 2 tablespoons Shawarma.
4. Serve hot with Tabbouleh and Hummus bi-tahini.

Fried Kibbi Balls
Akras al kibbi al maklieh

A famous dish loved by every member in the family.

Serves: 7
Preparation time: 1 hour
Cooking time: 30 minutes

Ingredients:

1 kg (32 oz) (5 cups) fine burghul (cracked wheat)
1 kg (32 oz) finely ground lean meat (ask for kibbi meat if available)
1 teaspoon salt
1 large onion
1 cup iced water or ice
¹/₂ teaspoon ground cinnamon
¹/₂ teaspoon ground allspice
6 cups vegetable oil (for deep fry)

Filling:
500 g (16 oz) minced meat
2 tablespoons shortening or butter
5 medium onions, finely chopped
1 cup fried pine nuts
¹/₂ teaspoon ground black pepper
¹/₄ teaspoon salt
a dash of ground cinnamon
a dash of ground allspice

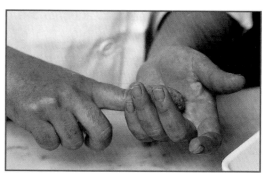

Steps:

1. Wash burghul under running water then soak in water for about 10 minutes. Drain then press to remove moisture as much as possible.
2. Mash onion in the food processor then add minced meat in batches. Remove and place aside.
3. Mix meat mixture with burghul, salt, allspice, and cinnamon. Process well in batches into a firm paste.
4. Knead mixture with wet hands into a smooth paste. Put in refrigerator for 30 minutes covered with a piece of wet texture.
5. **Filling**: Fry chopped onion with a dash of salt in shortening until transparent. Add minced meat, salt and spices to onions and fry until cooked. Mix in pine nuts. Put the filling aside.

6. Divide paste into balls (size of an egg). Dip your hands in cold water then roll each ball between the palms of your hands until smooth.
7. Make a hole in the middle with your forefinger.
8. Work finger round in the hole until you have a shell of even thickness.
9. Fill hole with filling mixture and close opening.
10. Moisten with cold water to seal well and to shape with two pointed sides. If any breaks appear in shell, close with wet fingers.
11. Place the balls on a tray. Heat oil in a pan then fry till brown evenly and cooked.
12. Serve kibbi hot with salads and yoghurt.

Note: you can use a special machine to form kibbi balls.

Roasted Lamb

Oozi (kharuf mahchi)

Oozi is perfect for big banquets and weddings.

Serves: 20
Preparation time: 1 $^1/_2$ hours
Cooking time: 5 hours

Ingredients:

*12-14 kg (348 - 488 oz) small lamb (cleaned from
  inside)*
2 kg (64 oz) minced meat
12 cups long grain rice, washed and drained
24 cups water
1 tablespoon salt (as desired)
1 $^1/_2$ cups blanched and flaked, fried almonds
$^1/_2$ cup fried pine nuts
1 $^1/_2$ cups blanched, fried pistachio nuts
1 tablespoon ground cinnamon
1 tablespoon ground allspice
1 tablespoon ground black pepper
1 tablespoon ground nutmeg
2 tablespoons ground white pepper
1 tablespoon ground cardamom
1 cup vegetable oil and butter mixture
*1 cup shortening or butter (for frying minced
  meat)*
Lemon wedges

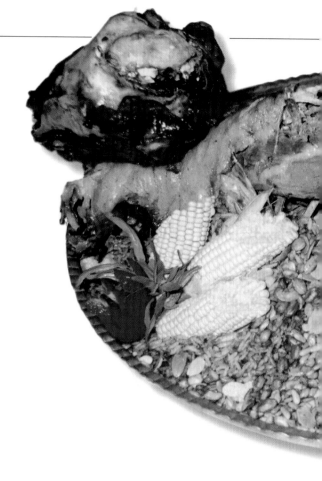

Steps:

1. Fry meat in 1 cup of shortening in a pot. Add salt
   and spices (except white pepper). Stir on medium
   heat until cooked.
2. Stir in rice to cooked meat. Add water. Bring to a
   boil. Cover pot and cook on low heat for 30 minutes.
3. Wipe lamb inside and out with a damp cloth. Rub
   cavity and outer surface with lemon wedges and
   white pepper.
4. Stuff lamb with half the quantity of rice. Stitch
   opening. Fry with oil and butter from all sides
   until golden.

5. Place aluminum foil on a big tray leaving extra on each side. Place the stuffed lamb on the foil. Pour 3 cups of water over.
6. Truss lamb legs with its shoulders using a firm rope. Wrap lamb generously with the foil.
7. Place the tray in high heat oven (220°C) for 5 hours, or until tender when pierced but still moist inside (add water if foil burns).
8. Remove lamb from oven. Open aluminum foil. Lift up slowly. Place on large serving platter. Arrange rice and meat around it. Garnish rice with pistachio nuts, almonds and pine nuts.
9. Serve hot accompanied with yoghurt and salads.

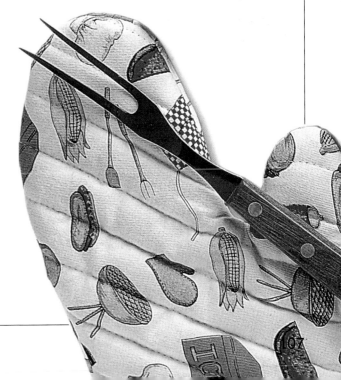

Shawarma

One of the most popular dishes, spread out around the world. It is best eaten as a sandwich.

Serves: 5
Preparation: 30 minutes
Cooking time: 1 hour

Ingredients:

1 kg (32 oz) fillets cut into strips (7 cm length 3 cm thickness)
200 g (7 oz) finely minced fat
2 large onions, peeled and sliced
¹/₄ cup vegetable oil
¹/₂ cup vinegar
¹/₂ tablespoon salt
1 tablespoon ground 7 spices for Shawarma

a dash of ground mastic
1 teaspoon ground nutmeg
1 teaspoon cardamom pods

Steps:

1. Soak sliced meat in 7 spices, salt, cardamom, mastic, nutmeg, vinegar, and oil for one night.
2. Fry fat in a heavy pan on medium heat. When it melts, add meat. Stir until golden. Add onion, cover and leave on low heat for 40 minutes or until tender.
3. Serve Shawarma hot with mint leaves, "taratour" and tomato slices.

Shawarma Sandwich Ingredients:

4 tablespoons cooked hot Shawarma
2 tablespoons finely chopped parsley
2 tablespoons roughly chopped tomato
1 teaspoon finely chopped onion
1 tablespoon chopped pickled cucumber
6 green mint leaves
2 tablespoons taratour
1 small pita bread

Steps:

1. Open a loaf of Arabic bread (pita), spread taratour over the inner side of the bread.
2. Spread Shawarma lengthwise, then sprinkle mint, parsley, tomatoes, onion and pickles over.
3. Roll loaf neatly and serve hot.

Stuffed Lamb Neck

Rakaba mahshiya

A delicious and nutritious main meal, served in special occasions.

Serves: 5
Preparation time: 1 hour 15 minutes
Cooking time: 2 hours 15 minutes

Ingredients:

1 lamb neck (2 kg / 64 oz), boned and cleaned
2 cups long rice, washed
300 g (10 oz) minced meat
¹/₂ cup shortening or butter
2 teaspoons salt
1 teaspoon ground allspice
1 teaspoon ground cinnamon
3 bay leaves
1 nutmeg
2 cloves
1 cinnamon stalk
2 medium onions, peeled
¹/₂ cup fried pine nuts
¹/₂ cup peeled and fried almonds
¹/₄ cup fried pistachio nuts
4 cups water

Steps:

1. Fry minced meat with half quantity of shortening for 10 minutes on low heat. Stir in rice for 1 minute. Add water and half quantity of salt, cinnamon, and allspice. Cook on low heat for 15 minutes. Remove half quantity of rice. Cook the rest for 15 minutes.
2. Stuff neck with half cooked rice. Stitch. Place in a pot. Add bay leaves, nutmeg, cloves and cinnamon stalk. Cover with water. Cook for 1 hour and 30 minutes.
3. Remove from pot. Brush with half the quantity of shortening. Place in an oven tray. Add spices and onion.
4. Place in a high heat oven (250°C-500°F) for 45 minutes. Turn to brown from all sides.
5. Serve in a large platter with the rest of the rice and meat mixture. Garnish with nuts.

Kabab Fingers

Asabih Kabab

Kabab fingers are made of parsley, onion, and bread.

Serves: 3
Preparation time: 15 minutes
Cooking time: 15 minutes

Ingredients:

500 g (16 oz) finely minced lean meat
2 tablespoons chopped fresh parsley
1 medium grated onion
2 tablespoons shortening or butter
1 teaspoon salt
¹/₂ teaspoon ground sweet pepper

Steps:

1. Blend meat, parsley, grated onion, salt, and pepper.
2. Divide meat mixture into equal pieces as big as a walnut. Make from each piece a finger shape piece.
3. Fry fingers with shortening until golden brown evenly.
4. Serve hot with salad or yoghurt.

> *Note: If you want, grill the fingers.*

Shish Kabab

Lahem mashwi

An Arabian - Style meat skewers.

Serves: 10
Preparation time: 30 minutes
Cooking time: 30 minutes

Ingredients:

2 kg (64 oz) lamb meat, cubed (5 cm)
6 small firm red tomatoes sliced
¹/₂ kg (16 oz) lard, chopped
1 tablespoon vegetable oil
7 small onions, peeled and halved
1 tablespoon salt
1 teaspoon ground allspice
1 teaspoon ground black pepper
1 teaspoon ground cinnamon
2 medium green bell peppers, chopped into medium pieces
¹/₂ cup finely chopped parsley
charcoal

Steps:

1. Mix meat with onion, spices, salt, lard, parsley, and oil. Place in refrigerator for 4 hours tossing occasionally.
2. Meanwhile prepare charcoal. Thread meat, onion, tomatoes, bell peppers onto skewers, alternating the ingredients.
3. Grill over hot coals. Turning several times until tender and browned, about 8 minutes.
4. Serve hot with salads and appetizers.

Note: If you use bamboo skewers, soak in water for 1 hour before using to keep the exposed portions from burning.

Golden Lamb Leg with Vegetables

Fakhda mohammara maa al khodar

This dish is perfect for a special occasion such as a birthday or a wedding anniversary.

Serves: 5
Preparation time: 30 minutes
Cooking time: 4 1/2 hours

Ingredients:

3 kg (96 oz) lamb leg
7 cloves garlic, peeled
1 kg (32 oz) golden baby potatoes, peeled, boiled
1 kg (32 oz) carrots, peeled, chopped, cooked
1 kg (32 oz) string beans, cooked
1 large onion, peeled
3 stalks celery or parsley, chopped
1/2 tablespoon ground black pepper
1/2 tablespoon ground white pepper
1 cinnamon stick
2 bay leaves
1 tablespoon salt
1/2 cup vegetable oil and butter mixture
1/2 tablespoon ground allspice

Steps:

1. Remove the outer thin transparent layer of leg. Rub leg with salt and allspice. Place in refrigerator for 1 night.
2. Fry leg in oil and butter mixture with onion, garlic, celery, some chopped carrots, white pepper and black pepper.
3. Heat oven to (250°C-500°F). Place leg with onion mixture, bay leaves, and cinnamon sticks in a large deep oven tray. Add 1 cup water and wrap with aluminum foil.
4. Lower heat to (200°C-400°F). Keep for 4 hours or until tender.
5. Remove leg from stock. Put aside until cool and can be carved.
6. Carve into lengthwise slices.
7. Drain leg's stock, add 1 tablespoon cornflour. Bring to a boil on medium heat until it thickens.
8. Serve leg garnished with cooked vegetables and pour over hot stock.

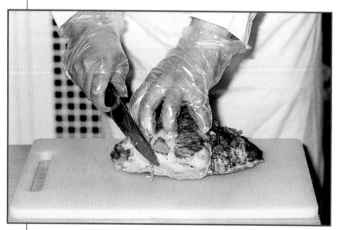

Baked Kibbi

Kibbi bil sanieh

Kibbi is the number one main meal or appetizer in the Levant. Whether cooked, fried, grilled, or raw it is delicious. When you taste it you'll ask for more.

Serves: 10

Preparation time: 2 hours

Cooking time: 30 minutes

Ingredients:

$^1/_2$ *kg (16 oz) ground lean meat*
$^1/_2$ *kg (16 oz) (2 $^1/_2$ cups) burghul smooth cracked wheat, washed*
$^1/_2$ *teaspoon ground allspice (as desired)*
$^1/_2$ *teaspoon ground cinnamon*
1 teaspoon salt
$^1/_2$ *cup finely chopped onion*
$^1/_2$ *cup vegetable oil and butter mixture*
$^1/_4$ *cup shortening, or butter (for greasing oven tray)*
Filling:
1 cup finely chopped onion
$^1/_2$ *kg (16 oz) minced meat*
1 cup shortening or butter
1 teaspoon salt
$^1/_2$ *teaspoon ground allspice*
a dash of black pepper
1 cup fried pine nuts

Steps:

1. **Filling**: Sauté onion with shortening over medium heat. Stir in meat, salt, and spices. Cook for 15 minutes till tender. Remove from heat. Mix in pine nuts.

2. Drain Burghul using a sieve, then press to remove excess water as much as possible.
   Process twice: meat and onion using a food processor. Remove meat mixture. Knead meat and burghul with your hands. Process meat mixture another time in the food processor. Remove, add salt and spices. Knead another time with wet palms (use cold water).

3. Divide meat mixture into two, make from each 4 balls.

4. Flatten each ball between your wet palms (use cold water). Place the 4 flattened balls in a greased oven tray (40x50 cm). Spread the 4 balls evenly using your wet palms (about 3 cm thick).

5. Spread filling over meat as steps 5,6. Cover filling with rest of the meat mixture repeating the same procedure as steps 3-4.

6. Run a knife blade around edge of tray, then score deeply into diamond shapes. Pour oil and shortening over top.

7. Bake in a moderate heat oven (200ºC-400ºF) for 30 minutes. Serve hot with salads and appetizers.

Baked Kafta
Kafta bil sanieh

One of the most famous easy to prepare dishes.

Serves: 5
Preparation time: 30 minutes
Cooking time: 20 minutes

Ingredients:

1 kg (32 oz) ground meat
¼ cup finely minced onion
1 cup finely chopped fresh parsley
1 kg (32 oz) potatoes, peeled and sliced (medium size)
fried round eggplant slices
2 medium onions, peeled and sliced
½ teaspoon ground cinnamon
½ teaspoon salt
½ teaspoon ground allspice
1 kg (32 oz) tomatoes, peeled and sliced
½ cup shortening or butter
1 cup vegetable oil
2 tablespoons pomegranate thickened juice
1 cup water

Steps:

1. Process minced onion and ground meat in food processor. Knead meat and onion with parsley, spices, and salt. Process meat mixture another time in food processor until smooth. Grease an oven tray (diameter 30 cm).
2. First way: Knead meat mixture another time. Divide meat mixture into balls (as desired) or shape into fingers. Fry in shortening until golden. Arrange in the tray.
   Second way: Spread meat mixture evenly in a greased tray using the palm of your hands. Bake in a moderate heat (180°C-350°F) oven for 7 minutes or until kafta is golden.
3. Fry potatoes in oil until nearly cooked. Arrange onions, eggplant, and potatoes over the meat in the tray.
4. Top with tomato slices. Pour 1 cup of water. Sprinkle salt. Cover and return to oven until kafta is cooked for about 20 minutes.
5. Serve hot accompanied with salads.

Lamb Leg with Truffles

Fakhda maa al kamaa

A main and nutritious dish served in special occasions.

Serves: 5
Preparation time: 30 minutes
Cooking time: 3 hours 30 minutes

Ingredients:

1 kg (32 oz) frozen truffles
3 kg (96 oz) lamb leg
1 tablespoon salt (as desired)
1/2 tablespoon ground black pepper
1/2 tablespoon ground white pepper
a dash of ground allspice
a dash of ground cinnamon
1 medium onion, peeled and finely chopped
2 medium onions, peeled
3 stalks celery or parsley, chopped
3 bay leaves
1 tablespoon cornflour dissolved in 1/4 cup water
2 liters water
1/2 cup vegetable oil and butter (or shortening) mixture

Steps:

1. Remove the outer thin transparent layer of leg. Rub leg with salt, allspice, and white pepper. Place in refrigerator for 1 night.

2. Fry in oil and butter with 2 onions, cinnamon, and black pepper.

3. Cover with water. Add celery, bay leaves. Cover pot and cook on medium heat for 3 hours or until tender.

4. Place frozen truffles in boiling water for minutes. Remove and place in cold water for 15 minutes.

5. Peel using a sharp knife. Cover with water. Add a dash of salt. Bring to a boil for 1 minute to be sure truffles are clean.

6. Slice truffles. Sauté chopped onion with some shortening. Stir in truffles slices for 7 minutes.

7. Remove half the quantity of leg's stock. Strain. Add cornflour dissolved in water to stock. Bring to a boil on medium heat until it thickens. Add fried onion and truffles to stock. Cook for 10 minutes.

8. Serve leg with truffle's sauce accompanied with brown rice.

Kibbi Balls in Yoghurt

Kibbi bi laban

Yoghurt has been consumed in the Middle East for centuries, making it the most ancient food known. This recipe is a combination of Kibbi and Yoghurt.

Serves: 10
Preparation time: 1 hour 30 minutes
Cooking time:1 hour

Ingredients:

500 g (16 oz) lean beef or lamb, finely ground
2 ¹/₂ cups fine burghul (cracked wheat)
1 medium onion, finely chopped
1 teaspoon salt
¹/₄ teaspoon ground black pepper
cold water for kneading
¹/₂ teaspoon ground allspice
¹/₂ teaspoon ground cinnamon
Filling:
500 g (16 oz) minced meat
1 large onion, finely chopped
1 teaspoon salt
¹/₄ cup fried pine nuts
¹/₄ teaspoon ground black pepper
Yoghurt mixture:
2 kg (64 oz) yoghurt
2 tablespoons cornflour
1 teaspoon salt
¹/₄ cup short grain rice
3 cloves garlic, crushed
1 cup finely chopped fresh coriander
¹/₄ cup shortening or butter
1 cup water (for rice)
1 egg, beaten

Steps:

1. Prepare Kibbi balls (see p.158 steps 1-10). Bake in an oven for 10 minutes.
2. Prepare cooked yoghurt (p.13).
3. In the meantime boil rice in water for 25 minutes. Stir in to boiling yoghurt.
4. Add Kibbi balls one by one (don't stir). Cook for 10 minutes over medium heat.
5. Fry garlic and coriander till fragrant. Add to Kibbi mixture. Cook for 3 minutes.
6. Pour in large bowls. Serve hot or cold.

Note: you can fry kibbi balls instead of baking it before adding it to cooked yoghurt.

Fried Sardines

Sardine Makli

For this recipe choose the tiny Sardine (about 4 cms long). Fry well till it becomes crunchy. Enjoy eating it without removing bones.

Serves: 4
Preparation time: 20 minutes
Cooking time: 30 minutes

Ingredients:

1 kg (32 oz) tiny sardines, cleaned
1 tablespoon salt
lemon wedges
1 cup vegetable oil (use another cup if necessary)

Steps:

1. Rub sardines with salt.
2. Put aside for 10 minutes until the salt is absorbed.
3. Fry in hot oil over medium heat, in batches, till brown. Remove with a slotted spoon.
4. Serve hot with lemon wedges.

Fish with Bell Pepper Sauce

Samke harra trabulsiya

A wonderful fish dish from the North of Lebanon.

Serves: 5
Preparation time: 45 minutes
Cooking time: 30 minutes

Ingredients:

1 kg (32 oz) fried or grilled fish, flaked
1 cup finely chopped onion
1 cup finely chopped green bell pepper
¹/₂ cup finely chopped coriander
¹/₂ cup ground pine nuts, almonds, and pistachio nuts
3 cups sesame paste sauce (Taratour)
1 tablespoon dried coriander
a dash of ground paprika
¹/₂ teaspoon ground chili (red pepper)
¹/₂ teaspoon ground cumin
¹/₂ cup olive oil
¹/₂ teaspoon salt

Steps:

1. Fry in hot oil onion, bell pepper, and coriander until soft.
2. Stir in spices, salt, and ground nuts.
3. Pour sesame paste sauce over the mixture, stir constantly on medium heat until the oil's bubbles appears and the mixture thickens.
4. Pour mixture in serving platter. Garnish with fish flakes, lemon wedges, fried pine nuts and some chopped parsley.

Grilled Fish

Al Samak al mashwi

This fish recipe makes an excellent summer lunch.

Serves: 4
Preparation time: 35 minutes
Cooking time: 1 hour

Ingredients:

1 large-sized fish (about 2
kg/64 oz), cleaned
lemon wedges
¹/₄ teaspoon ground cumin
1 finely chopped leek stalk
¹/₄ cup finely chopped fresh parsley or finely
chopped celery stalk
¹/₂ cup vegetable oil or olive oil
¹/₄ teaspoon ground white pepper
2 tablespoons salt (as desired)

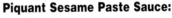

Steps:

1. Rub fish with salt and spices. Put aside.
2. Mix leek, parsley and lemon wedges. Stuff fish with leek mixture.
3. Pour half quantity of oil on an aluminum foil. Put fish on it. Pour over remaining oil. Wrap completely with foil.
4. Pour some water in an oven tray. Put the fish wrapped with foil on the tray. Place the tray inside a moderate heat oven (200°C/400°F) for 1 hour or until tender. Remove leek mixture.
5. Serve with Taratour or piquant sesame paste sauce.

Piquant Sesame Paste Sauce:

Mix 1 cup sesame paste with 1 cup of water and 1 cup of lemon juice. Fry 1 medium finely chopped onion in oil on medium heat. Stir in 5 crushed cloves garlic and 1 teaspoon dried coriander for 1 minute. Stir in for another 7 minutes, ground walnuts and sesame paste mixture. When it boils, add ¹/₂ teaspoon ground red pepper. Cook on low heat until the mixture thickens slightly and you see sesame paste oil appears on top of mixture.

Lebanese Garlic Fish

Samke harra bil al toum wa al kizbara

It is considered the most popular fish recipe in Lebanon. Try it, you will love it.

Serves: 5
Preparation time: 30 minutes
Cooking time: 35 minutes

Ingredients:

1 large fish (about 2 kg/64 oz), cleaned, scaled, rubbed inside and out with salt
1/4 cup vegetable oil
2 heads garlic, peeled and sliced
7 cups finely chopped fresh coriander
1/2 cup finely chopped onion
1/2 cup fried pine nuts
1 tablespoon vinegar
a dash of ground dried coriander
a dash of piquant red pepper
a dash of ground cumin
3/4 cup lemon juice
salt as desired

Steps:

1. Fry fish in 1 cup hot oil over medium heat till golden on both sides. Reduce heat and fry till tender.
2. Remove bones. Put meat in a platter.
3. Fry chopped onion in 1/4 cup oil till soft. Stir in garlic, dry coriander, cumin, pepper and salt.
4. Add lemon juice, vinegar, and some water to onion mixture. Cook until mixture thickens. Stir in for 1 minute green coriander and half the quantity of fish. Remove from heat.
5. Serve in a platter garnished with fried pine nuts and lemon wedges.

Fried Fish
Sharaeh al Samak al makli

Fish tastes best when it is fried. What makes difference is the way you fry it and what you serve with it.

Serves: 4
Preparation time: 30 minutes
Cooking time: 30 minutes

Ingredients:

2 kg (64 oz) white fish, cleaned and scaled, cut into fillets
2 cups vegetable oil
¹/₂ tablespoon salt
2 tablespoons flour (as desired)
lemon wedges, peeled and seeded

Steps:

1. Wipe fish dry and rub from the both sides with salt. Refrigerate for 30 minutes. Coat fish with flour.
2. Heat oil in a pan. Fry fish over medium heat (see that oil covers fish). When golden brown, turn on the other side. Lower heat and fry till tender. Put on absorbent papers.
3. Serve fish hot, garnished with lemon wedges and parsley. Serve accompanied with salads, sesame seed sauce and fried pita pieces.

Note: You can fry pita in fish oil till golden-brown, and serve it with any fish dish.

Lebanese Fish and Rice

Sayyadiat al samak

Fish is always a great main meal. This recipe is tasty and won't keep you long in the kitchen.

Serves: 6
Preparation time: 30 minutes
Cooking time: 1 hour

Ingredients:

1 fish (1 kg/32 oz), cleaned and fried or grilled,
* flaked (reserve head)*
1 ¹/₂ cups vegetable oil
7 medium onions, roughly chopped
2 teaspoons salt
2 cups long grain rice, washed and drained
5 cups boiled water
1 tablespoon lemon juice
a dash of white pepper and cumin
¹/₂ cup fried pine nuts

Steps:

1. Heat oil in a deep pot. Fry fish's head until golden. Remove from oil.
2. Fry onion until golden in ¹/₂ cup of the oil in which the fish's head has been fried in.
3. Add fish's head, salt, cumin, and pepper to onion. Cover with water. Cook on high heat until it boils. Lower heat to moderate and cook for 30 minutes.
4. Remove the fish's head. Strain stock. Add rice and lemon juice to stock. Bring to a boil.
5. Lower heat and cook for 20 minutes. Serve rice in a platter.
6. Garnish platter with flaked fish and pine nuts.

Ground Fish

Akras al samak bil kaek

Delicious and good for the whole family.

Serves: 4
Preparation time: 1 hour
Cooking time: 15 minutes

Ingredients:

750 g (24 oz) firm white fish fillets, cut into strips, each 2x5 cm
1 teaspoon finely grated lime rind
1 egg, beaten with a dash of ground white pepper
1 teaspoon salt (as desired)
2 teaspoons chopped fresh coriander
vegetable oil for deep frying
$\frac{1}{2}$ cup milk
$\frac{1}{2}$ cup flour
$\frac{1}{2}$ cup dried breadcrumbs

Steps:

1. Place breadcrumbs, coriander, salt, and lime rind in a small bowl and mix to combine.
2. Dip each fillet in milk, then in flour, egg, and finally in breadcrumb mixture.
3. Place fillets on a plate lined with plastic food wrap, cover and chill for at least 30 minutes.
4. Heat oil in a large, deep sauce pan and cook fillets in batches for 2-3 minutes or until golden.
5. Using a slotted spoon remove fillets and drain on absorbent kitchen paper.
6. Serve hot garnished with parsley and lemon wedges.

Banana and Milk Juice

Sharab al haleeb maa al moz

A delicious and easy to prepare juice.

Serves: 5
Preparation time: 10 minutes

Ingredients:

3 bananas
1 cup fresh cold milk
¼ cup strawberry juice
¼ cup sugar or honey (as desired)

Steps:

1. Mash banana in a food processor.
2. Stir in milk, sugar, and strawberry juice.
3. Serve it in the mornings to your children.

Cocktail Drink

Sharab mshakkal

A nutritious drink made from fresh fruits.

Makes about: 4 cups
Preparation time: 15 minutes

Ingredients:

³⁄₄ cup fresh strawberry juice
³⁄₄ cup mango juice
³⁄₄ cup guava or pineapple juice
³⁄₄ cup apple juice
2 small bananas, cut each into 8 pieces
4 small peach slices
4 strawberries, washed
4 tablespoons honey
¼ cup fresh milk
¼ cup blanched and ground almonds
¼ cup ground pistachio nuts

4 tablespoons fresh cream
2 pineapple slices, chopped into16 pieces
2 teaspoons sugar (as desired)

Steps:

1. Place strawberry, mango, guava and apple juices in a blender. Blend in milk, honey, sugar, almonds, and pistachio nuts.
2. Prepare 4 cups. Add to each cup 4 pieces of banana, 1 slice of peach, and 4 pieces of pineapple.
3. Pour fruit juices mixture in glasses. Garnish with 1 tablespoon of cream and 1 strawberry.
4. Serve cold.

Liquorice Roots Juice

Sharab aruk al sous

A cold and delicious juice. Perfect for the fasting in the holly month of Ramadan.

Serves: 12
Preparation time: 1 hour

Ingredients:

$^1/_2$ kg (16 oz) ground liquorice roots
1 teaspoon bicarbonate of soda
15 cups of water
Sugar as (desired)
a piece of muslin
grated ice

Steps:

1. Place ground liquorice in a piece of muslin. Add $^1/_2$ quantity of bicarbonate of soda.
2. Pour 4 cups of water in liquorice. Rub well until the color of liquid becomes dark.
3. Add the remaining quantity of bicarbonate of soda. Tie the muslin to form a bag on a bowl.
4. Pour water and turn over the bag from time to time. Place in the refrigerator for 6 to 8 hours.
5. Serve cold sweeted with sugar. Sprinkle on top some grated ice.

Turkish Coffee

Kahwa turkiya

Almost every person in the Arab world must have an early cup of Turkish coffee before starting the day.

Serves: 1

Preparation time: 2 minutes

Ingredients:

1 ¼ tiny Arabic coffee cup of water
½ teaspoon sugar (according to taste)
1 teaspoonful ground coffee mixed with ground cardamom
(bought with or without cardamom according to taste)

Steps:

1. Put water in a kettle over medium heat, add sugar, coffee and keep stirring till mixture boils.
2. Reduce heat and keep boiling by moving kettle on and off for 1 minute.
3. Serve hot.

White Coffee

Kahwa bayda

This coffee is usually served after heavy meals.

Serves: 1

Preparation time: 2 minutes

Ingredients:

1 Tiny Arabic coffee cup water
1 teaspoon orange flower water
2 cardamom pods
½ teaspoon sugar

Steps:

1. Put water in a kettle over medium heat. Add sugar. Stir till dissolved. Add orange flower water and cardamom pods. Boil for 1 minute by moving kettle on and off heat.
2. Serve hot.

GLOSSARY

ALLSPICE
Though it is a spice from the new world, allspice has been adopted in Middle East cooking for its similarity to the combined flavors of clove, cinnamon and nutmeg. Commonly referred to as "bahar".

BURGHUL
Hulled wheat, steamed until partly cooked, dried then ground. Available in fine and coarse grades. Recipes specify which grade to use. It has a nut-like flavor making it a popular food for those following natural food diets. It is widely used in Lebanon, Syria and neighboring countries. Available at Middle East, Greek and Armenian food stores and specialty food stores.

CARAWAY
Caraway is originally from the countries of temperate Asia, including Iran and Turkey. It has been used as a spice for 5,000 years. A biennial plant, caraway grows up to 60 cm in height with feathery leaves and creamy white flowers. It comes in different forms: dried ground leaves, fresh tap roots, and dried seeds. Purchase from Middle East and Armenian food's stores.

CARDAMOM
(Cardamon, Cardamum)
Native to Asia and South America, Cardamom is the dried fruit of a plant (Elettaria Cardamum) belonging to the ginger family. The pods are cream-colored and the seeds inside are brownish-black. The spice is bitter-sweet, very aromatic and has a slightly Lemony aftertaste. Ground cardamom is widely used in Scandinavian, Eastern and Italian dishes and is also one of the ingredients in curry powder. The seeds are sometimes used whole in pickling spice and marinades.

CUMIN

Middle Eastern spice with a strong, dusky, aromatic flavor, popular in cuisines of its region of origin. Sold either as whole, small, crescent-shaped seeds, or ground.

KAHWA , (Turkish Coffee)

In the Middle East every household has its rakwi (long-handled coffee pot). To impress your Arabic host or your guests, know the right coffee talk-*murrah* for sugarless coffee, *mazboutah* for medium sweet and *hilweh* for very sweet. Coffee is always served in tiny, bowl-shaped cups. To each Arabic coffee cup measure of water, add a level teaspoon sugar for medium sweet, a heaped teaspoon for very sweet. Stir sugar in water over heat until dissolved and boiling. Add 1 heaped teaspoon pulverized coffee (usually a dark roasted coffee) for each cup water, stir well and cook until foam rises to the top of the pot. The pot is removed from the heat and the base rapped on a flat surface to reduce foaming. Heat twice more, with raps in between. Pour immediately into the cups. To flavor the coffee, cardamom pods are ground with the beans (3 or 4 with each 250g or 8 oz beans). Traditionally few drops of orange blossom water would be added to individual taste.

LOOMI, (Dried Limes)

They are necessary flavor additive to gulf cooking and are also used in Iran and Iraq. While the Gulf cooks use Loomi either whole or powdered, they are only used whole in Iran and Iraq. When using them intact, they must be pierced with a skewer or fork on each side so the cooking liquid can travel through the lime to take the flavor.

MARJORAM

A herb native to Western Asia and to Mediterranean. The gray-green leaves are dried and are slightly aromatic with minty overtones.

MISTICHA / MASTIC, Arabic: (Mistiki)

Misticha is a resin from a small ever green tree, with most of the world's supply coming from the Greek island of Chios. From ancient times it has been used as a chewing gum. The powdered resin is used to flavor sweet breads. In Egypt a small piece of misticha is often added to boiling chicken to remove unwanted flavors.

POMEGRANATE THICKENED JUICE

To juice the fruit, place a handful of seeds at a time in a muslin bag and squeeze juice into a bowl. Freeze in ice-cube trays, then pack cubes in plastic bags and store in freezer. If fresh pomegranate juice is not available, use pomegranate molasses or syrup, *dibs roman*, available at Middle East food stores. Use 3-4 teaspoons *dibs roman* in 1 cup water for 1 cup pomegranate juice.

SAFFRON, Arabic: Zaaffaran

It is the world's most expensive spice. It takes the stamens almost a quarter million blooms to produce 500g (16 oz) of saffron. The use of saffron originated in Asia Minor in ancient times. Buy a reliable brand as there are cheaper versions sold which are not true saffron. Pound threads in a mortar and soak in liquid specified to bring out the fragrance and color.

SESAME PASTE / TAHINI, (Taheena, Tahina)

A Middle Eastern sesame seed paste similar in consistency to mayonnaise and used in the preparation of *hummus*. Tahina by itself is spooned on to small plates in the same way as *hummus*, garnished with a sprinkle of olive oil, black olives and chopped parsley and eaten with pieces of pitta bread as an appetizer.

SUMAC

The dried, crushed red berries of a species of sumac tree. It has a pleasant sour taste, rather lemony in flavor. It is advisable that sumac be purchased at Middle East and Armenian food stores.

SWEET PEPPER , Arabic: BIHAR HOLOU

Powdered spice derived from the dried pepper; available in sweet, mild and hot forms. Buy in small quantities from shops with high turnover, to ensure a fresh, flavorful supply.